From Misunderstood To Mainstream

Travis Breeding

Published by Travis Breeding, 2024.

FROM MISUNDERSTOOD TO MAINSTREAM

First edition. February 20, 2024.

ISBN: 979-8224998814

Written by Travis Breeding.

Also by Travis Breeding

Harmony in Flux: Navigating Bi-Polar Brilliance
The Friendship Rainbow
The Great Kindergarten Adventure: A Story about Going to School with Autism
The Magic Forest Adventure
Unlocking Brilliance: Navigating Autism and Applied Behavior Analysis Towards a Radiant Future
Decoding Love: Navigating Dating and Relationships on the Autism Spectrum
Echoes of a Late Diagnosis: Unveiling the Spectrum Within
From Theory to Practice: Implementing Effective Autism Interventions St
The Amazing Adventures of Aiden and His Asperger's Superpowers
The Magical Adventures of Lily and the Enchanted Forest
Unlocking Potential: A Journey Of Discovery Through ABA Therapy
Unlocking Potential: Navigating Employment for Neurodiverse Talent
Unlocking the Spectrum: A Journey through Applied Behavior Analysis from an Autistic Perspective
Unlocking The Spectrum: Navigating The Complexity Of Autism With Advanced Strategies And Insights
Beyond The Spectrum: Insights From Autistic Adults
Beyond The Stereotypes
Breaking Barriers: Navigating Autism With Therapeutic Insight
Celebrating Neurodiversity

Embracing Differences
From Diagnosis To Treatment
From Dreams To Reality: The Young President
Living With Autism: A Journey Of Triumph And Challenges
Neurodiversity Unveiled: Navigating The Spectrum Of Inclusion
Sunshine At Disney World
The Art Of Reinforcement
The Magical School Bus Ride: A Journey Of Understanding
ThroughThe Spectrum Of Love
From Misunderstood To Mainstream

Watch for more at breedingautismconsulting.com.

Table of Contents

Chapter 1: Advanced Interventions for Autism

Autism Spectrum Disorder (ASD) is a neurodevelopmental disorder that affects individuals in various ways. It is characterized by difficulties in social interaction, communication, and repetitive behaviors. While there is no cure for ASD, there are advanced interventions available that can greatly improve the quality of life for individuals with this disorder. These interventions aim to address the specific challenges faced by individuals with ASD and help them develop skills and strategies to navigate the world more effectively.

Seeking advanced interventions for individuals with ASD is crucial because it can make a significant difference in their overall well-being and development. These interventions are designed to target the specific needs of individuals with ASD and provide them with the support and tools they need to thrive. By addressing the challenges associated with ASD early on, individuals can have a better chance of reaching their full potential and leading fulfilling lives.

Understanding Autism Spectrum Disorder and Its Challenges

Autism Spectrum Disorder is a complex neurodevelopmental disorder that affects individuals in different ways. It is characterized by difficulties in social interaction, communication, and repetitive behaviors. Individuals with ASD may have difficulty understanding social cues, expressing themselves verbally or non-verbally, and may engage in repetitive behaviors such as hand-flapping or rocking.

One of the main challenges faced by individuals with ASD is social interaction. They may struggle to understand social cues such as facial expressions, body language, and tone of voice. This can make it difficult for them to form meaningful relationships and navigate social situations effectively. Communication is another area of challenge for individuals with ASD. They may have difficulty expressing themselves verbally or understanding spoken language. This can lead to frustration and isolation.

Individualized interventions are crucial for individuals with ASD because each person's needs and challenges are unique. What works for one individual may not work for another. By tailoring interventions to the specific needs of each individual, professionals can provide targeted support that addresses their challenges and helps them develop the skills they need to succeed.

The Importance of Early Intervention and Diagnosis

Early intervention and diagnosis are crucial for individuals with ASD because they can greatly improve outcomes and quality of life. Research has shown that early intervention can lead to significant improvements in communication, social skills, and cognitive abilities for individuals with ASD. The earlier the intervention is provided, the better the chances of positive outcomes.

There are several signs and symptoms that may indicate the presence of ASD. These can include delayed speech or language skills, difficulty with social interactions, repetitive behaviors, and sensory sensitivities. It is important for parents and caregivers to be aware of these signs and seek professional help if they suspect their child may have ASD.

Seeking professional help for diagnosis and intervention is essential because it allows individuals with ASD to receive the support and resources they need to thrive. Professionals can conduct comprehensive assessments to determine if an individual has ASD and develop a personalized intervention plan based on their specific needs. Early intervention can provide individuals with the tools and strategies they need to navigate the challenges associated with ASD and reach their full potential.

Behavioral Interventions for Autism Spectrum Disorder

Behavioral interventions are a common approach used in the treatment of Autism Spectrum Disorder. These interventions focus on modifying behaviors and teaching new skills to individuals with ASD. They are based on the principles of applied behavior analysis (ABA) and aim to increase desired behaviors while decreasing challenging behaviors.

There are several examples of behavioral interventions that can be effective for individuals with ASD. One example is discrete trial training (DTT), which involves breaking down skills into smaller steps and using repetition and reinforcement to teach those skills. Another example is pivotal response training (PRT), which focuses on teaching pivotal skills such as motivation, self-management, and responding to multiple cues.

Behavioral interventions have been shown to have many benefits for individuals with ASD. They can help improve communication skills, social interactions, and adaptive behaviors. These interventions also provide individuals with the tools and strategies they need to navigate the challenges associated with ASD and lead more independent lives.

Cognitive Interventions for Autism Spectrum Disorder

Cognitive interventions focus on improving cognitive abilities such as attention, memory, problem-solving, and executive functioning in individuals with ASD. These interventions aim to enhance cognitive skills and help individuals with ASD develop strategies to overcome cognitive challenges.

There are several examples of cognitive interventions that can be effective for individuals with ASD. One example is cognitive behavioral therapy (CBT), which helps individuals identify and change negative thought patterns and behaviors. Another example is social thinking, which focuses on teaching individuals with ASD how to understand and interpret social cues.

Cognitive interventions have been shown to have many benefits for individuals with ASD. They can improve cognitive abilities, problem-solving skills, and executive functioning. These interventions also provide individuals with the tools and strategies they need to navigate the cognitive challenges associated with ASD and succeed in various areas of life.

Social Skills Interventions for Autism Spectrum Disorder

Social skills interventions are designed to help individuals with ASD develop the social skills they need to interact effectively with others. These interventions focus on teaching individuals how to understand social cues, initiate and maintain conversations, and develop meaningful relationships.

There are several examples of social skills interventions that can be effective for individuals with ASD. One example is social skills training, which involves teaching individuals specific social skills through modeling, role-playing, and practice. Another example is peer-mediated interventions, which involve pairing individuals with ASD with typically developing peers to facilitate social interactions.

Social skills interventions have been shown to have many benefits for individuals with ASD. They can improve social interactions, communication skills, and overall quality of life. These interventions also provide individuals with the tools and strategies they need to navigate social situations effectively and form meaningful relationships.

Communication Interventions for Autism Spectrum Disorder

Communication interventions are designed to help individuals with ASD improve their communication skills and abilities. These interventions focus on teaching individuals how to express themselves verbally or non-verbally, understand spoken language, and use alternative forms of communication.

There are several examples of communication interventions that can be effective for individuals with ASD. One example is speech therapy, which focuses on improving speech and language skills through various techniques and strategies. Another example is augmentative and alternative communication (AAC), which involves using tools and devices to support communication.

Communication interventions have been shown to have many benefits for individuals with ASD. They can improve communication skills, expressive and receptive language abilities, and overall quality of life. These interventions also provide individuals with the tools and strategies they need to effectively communicate their wants, needs, and thoughts.

Sensory Interventions for Autism Spectrum Disorder

Sensory interventions are designed to help individuals with ASD manage sensory sensitivities and challenges. Many individuals with ASD have heightened or diminished sensory responses, which can affect their ability to function in everyday environments. Sensory interventions aim to provide individuals with strategies to regulate their sensory experiences and navigate sensory-rich environments.

There are several examples of sensory interventions that can be effective for individuals with ASD. One example is sensory integration therapy, which involves engaging individuals in activities that stimulate their senses in a controlled and structured manner. Another example is the use of sensory tools such as weighted blankets or fidget toys to provide sensory input.

Sensory interventions have been shown to have many benefits for individuals with ASD. They can help individuals regulate their sensory experiences, reduce anxiety and stress, and improve overall functioning. These interventions also provide individuals with the tools and strategies they need to navigate sensory-rich environments more effectively.

Technology-Based Interventions for Autism Spectrum Disorder

Technology-based interventions are becoming increasingly popular in the treatment of Autism Spectrum Disorder. These interventions utilize technology such as computers, tablets, or smartphones to deliver therapeutic content and support individuals with ASD in various areas.

There are several examples of technology-based interventions that can be effective for individuals with ASD. One example is the use of social skills apps or programs that provide interactive and engaging activities to teach social skills. Another example is the use of virtual reality to create simulated environments for individuals to practice real-life situations.

Technology-based interventions have been shown to have many benefits for individuals with ASD. They can provide engaging and interactive learning experiences, increase motivation and participation, and improve overall outcomes. These interventions also provide individuals with the tools and strategies they need to navigate various areas of life using technology.

Medication-Based Interventions for Autism Spectrum Disorder

Medication-based interventions are sometimes used in the treatment of Autism Spectrum Disorder to manage specific symptoms or co-occurring conditions. These interventions aim to alleviate symptoms such as anxiety, hyperactivity, or aggression that may be interfering with an individual's functioning and well-being.

There are several examples of medication-based interventions that can be used for individuals with ASD. One example is the use of selective serotonin reuptake inhibitors (SSRIs) to manage anxiety or depression. Another example is the use of stimulant medications to manage hyperactivity or impulsivity.

Medication-based interventions can have benefits for individuals with ASD by reducing specific symptoms that may be interfering with their daily functioning. However, it is important to note that medication should always be used in conjunction with other interventions and under the guidance of a healthcare professional.

There are potential risks and side effects associated with medication use, so it is important to carefully weigh the benefits and risks before making a decision.

The Future of Advanced Interventions for Autism Spectrum Disorder

The field of advanced interventions for Autism Spectrum Disorder is constantly evolving, and there is ongoing research and development in this area. Researchers are exploring new approaches and technologies to improve outcomes for individuals with ASD and address their unique challenges.

One area of current research is the use of virtual reality (VR) as a therapeutic tool for individuals with ASD. VR can provide immersive and realistic experiences that allow individuals to practice real-life situations in a controlled and safe environment. This can be particularly beneficial for individuals with ASD who struggle with social interactions or sensory sensitivities.

Another area of research is the use of genetic testing to identify specific genetic markers associated with ASD. This can help healthcare professionals develop personalized interventions based on an individual's genetic profile, leading to more targeted and effective treatments.

Continued research and development of interventions for ASD is crucial to improve outcomes and quality of life for individuals with this disorder. By staying up-to-date with the latest advancements in the field, individuals with ASD and their families can make informed decisions about the interventions that may be most beneficial for them.

Seeking advanced interventions for individuals with Autism Spectrum Disorder is crucial because it can greatly improve their overall well-being and development. These interventions are designed to address the specific challenges faced by individuals with ASD and provide them with the support and tools they need to thrive.

Early intervention and diagnosis are particularly important because they can lead to better outcomes for individuals with ASD. By addressing the challenges associated with ASD early on, individuals can have a better chance of reaching their full potential and leading fulfilling lives.

There are various types of advanced interventions available for individuals with ASD, including behavioral, cognitive, social skills, communication, sensory, technology-based, and medication-based interventions. Each type of intervention targets specific areas of challenge and provides individuals with the tools and strategies they need to navigate those challenges effectively.

The future of advanced interventions for Autism Spectrum Disorder looks promising, with ongoing research and development in the field. Researchers are exploring new approaches and technologies to improve outcomes for individuals with ASD and address their unique challenges.

In conclusion, seeking advanced interventions for individuals with Autism Spectrum Disorder is crucial because it can make a significant difference in their overall well-being and development. By addressing the specific challenges associated with ASD and providing targeted support, individuals can have a better chance of reaching their full potential and leading fulfilling lives. It is important for individuals with ASD and their families to seek professional help for diagnosis and intervention to ensure they receive the support and resources they need.

Chapter 2: Autism Beyond Childhood: Challenges and Triumphs for Adults

Autism Spectrum Disorder (ASD) is a neurodevelopmental disorder that affects individuals in various ways. It is characterized by difficulties in social communication and interaction, as well as restricted and repetitive patterns of behavior, interests, or activities. While much attention has been given to children with ASD, it is equally important to understand and support adults with ASD.

Statistics on the prevalence of ASD in adults vary, but it is estimated that around 1% of the global population has ASD. However, the number of adults diagnosed with ASD may be underreported due to late or missed diagnoses. Many individuals may not receive a diagnosis until adulthood, which can make it challenging for them to access appropriate support and services.

Understanding and supporting adults with ASD is crucial for their overall well-being and quality of life. By recognizing their unique strengths and challenges, we can create a more inclusive society that values and supports individuals with ASD.

Understanding the Unique Challenges of Autism in Adulthood

Adults with ASD face a range of challenges that can impact their daily lives. These challenges include differences in social communication and interaction, sensory processing difficulties, executive functioning challenges, and co-occurring mental health conditions.

Social communication and interaction can be particularly challenging for adults with ASD. They may struggle with understanding social cues, maintaining eye contact, or engaging in reciprocal conversations. This can lead to difficulties in forming and maintaining relationships, both personal and professional.

Sensory processing difficulties are also common among adults with ASD. They may be hypersensitive or hyposensitive to certain sensory stimuli, such as noise, touch, or light. This can result in sensory overload or sensory seeking behaviors, which can be overwhelming and distressing.

Executive functioning refers to a set of cognitive processes that help individuals plan, organize, and complete tasks. Adults with ASD often struggle with executive functioning challenges, such as time management, organization, and problem-solving. These difficulties can impact their ability to navigate daily tasks and responsibilities.

Additionally, many adults with ASD also experience co-occurring mental health conditions, such as anxiety and depression. These conditions can further complicate their daily lives and require additional support and intervention.

Navigating Relationships and Social Interactions

Building and maintaining relationships can be challenging for adults with ASD, but there are strategies that can help. It is important to provide individuals with opportunities for social interaction and practice social skills. This can be done through structured social skills training programs or by participating in group activities or clubs that align with their interests.

Coping with social anxiety and sensory overload in social situations is another important aspect of navigating relationships. Adults with ASD may benefit from developing coping strategies, such as deep breathing exercises or taking breaks when feeling overwhelmed. It is also important for individuals to communicate their needs and boundaries to others, so they can feel more comfortable in social settings.

There are resources available for social skills training and support. Many organizations offer social skills groups or workshops specifically designed for individuals with ASD. These programs provide a safe and supportive environment for individuals to practice social skills and build relationships.

Finding Employment and Career Success

Finding employment and achieving career success can be challenging for adults with ASD due to the unique difficulties they face. Many individuals with ASD have strengths in areas such as attention to detail, problem-solving, and pattern recognition, which can be valuable in certain careers.

However, there are also challenges that adults with ASD may encounter in the workplace. These challenges include difficulties with social communication, sensory sensitivities, and executive functioning. It is important for employers to provide accommodations and supports to help individuals with ASD succeed on the job.

Accommodations can include providing a quiet workspace, allowing flexible work hours, or providing clear instructions and expectations. Employers can also offer training programs or mentorship opportunities to help individuals with ASD develop their skills and advance in their careers.

There are resources available for job training and employment assistance for individuals with ASD. Vocational rehabilitation programs, job coaches, and disability employment services can provide support and guidance in finding and maintaining employment.

Managing Sensory Overload in the Workplace

Sensory overload can be a significant challenge for adults with ASD in the workplace. Common triggers for sensory overload include loud noises, bright lights, strong smells, or crowded spaces. Sensory overload can lead to anxiety, stress, and difficulty concentrating.

There are strategies that individuals with ASD can use to manage sensory overload in the workplace. This may include using noise-canceling headphones, taking regular breaks in a quiet space, or using fidget toys to help regulate sensory input. It is important for individuals to communicate their needs to their employers and advocate for accommodations that can help them manage sensory overload.

Advocating for accommodations and modifications in the workplace is crucial for individuals with ASD. This may involve having open and honest conversations with employers or human resources departments about specific needs and challenges. By advocating for their needs, individuals with ASD can create a more supportive and inclusive work environment.

Coping with Anxiety and Depression

Anxiety and depression are common co-occurring mental health conditions among adults with ASD. The prevalence of anxiety and depression in this population is higher than in the general population. These conditions can significantly impact an individual's daily life and overall well-being.

There are strategies that individuals with ASD can use to manage anxiety and depression. These strategies may include practicing relaxation techniques, engaging in regular exercise, seeking therapy or counseling, or participating in support groups. It is important for individuals to reach out for professional help if needed and to develop a support network of friends, family, or peers who can provide emotional support.

There are resources available for mental health support for adults with ASD. Many organizations offer therapy services specifically tailored to individuals with ASD. These services can provide individuals with the tools and strategies they need to manage their anxiety and depression effectively.

Accessing Healthcare and Support Services

Accessing healthcare and support services can be challenging for adults with ASD. Many individuals face barriers such as lack of understanding from healthcare providers, limited access to specialized services, or difficulties navigating the healthcare system.

It is important for individuals with ASD to advocate for their healthcare and support needs. This may involve educating healthcare providers about their specific needs and challenges, seeking out specialized services or providers who have experience working with individuals with ASD, or reaching out to advocacy organizations for guidance and support.

There are resources available for finding and accessing appropriate healthcare and support services. Autism advocacy organizations can provide information and resources on healthcare providers, support groups, or other services that may be beneficial for adults with ASD.

Building Independent Living Skills

Developing independent living skills is crucial for adults with ASD to live fulfilling and independent lives. These skills include tasks such as managing finances, cooking, cleaning, personal hygiene, and transportation.

Strategies for building independent living skills may include breaking tasks down into smaller steps, using visual supports or schedules, practicing skills in a structured environment, or seeking out training programs or classes that focus on independent living skills.

There are resources available for independent living support. Many organizations offer programs or services specifically designed to help individuals with ASD develop independent living skills. These programs can provide guidance, support, and practical tools to help individuals become more self-sufficient.

Advocating for Autism Acceptance and Inclusion

Advocating for autism acceptance and inclusion is crucial for creating a more inclusive society that values and supports individuals with ASD. It is important to challenge stereotypes and misconceptions about autism and promote understanding and acceptance.

There are many ways to get involved in advocacy efforts. This may include participating in awareness campaigns, supporting autism organizations through donations or volunteering, or sharing personal stories and experiences to promote positive representation of individuals with ASD.

There are resources available for advocacy and activism. Autism advocacy organizations can provide information, resources, and guidance on how to get involved in advocacy efforts. By working together, we can create a more inclusive and accepting society for individuals with ASD.

Celebrating the Triumphs and Achievements of Adults with Autism

It is important to celebrate the triumphs and achievements of adults with ASD. By highlighting their successes, we can challenge stereotypes and promote a more positive and inclusive narrative about autism.

There are many examples of successful adults with ASD who have made significant contributions in various fields. These individuals serve as role models and inspiration for others with ASD. By sharing their stories, we can promote positive representation and encourage others to pursue their goals and dreams.

There are resources available for sharing success stories and promoting positive representation. Many organizations and websites feature stories of individuals with ASD who have achieved success in various areas. These resources can provide inspiration and encouragement for individuals with ASD and their families.

The Importance of Supporting Adults with Autism

Understanding and supporting adults with ASD is crucial for their overall well-being and quality of life. By recognizing their unique strengths and challenges, we can create a more inclusive society that values and supports individuals with ASD.

Adults with ASD face a range of challenges, including differences in social communication and interaction, sensory processing difficulties, executive functioning challenges, and co-occurring mental health conditions. However, there are strategies, resources, and supports available to help them navigate these challenges and live fulfilling lives.

It is important for individuals with ASD to advocate for their needs, access appropriate support services, and develop independent living skills. By celebrating the triumphs and achievements of adults with ASD, we can challenge stereotypes and promote a more positive narrative about autism.

In conclusion, supporting adults with ASD is not only beneficial for individuals with ASD themselves but also for society as a whole. By creating a more inclusive and accepting society, we can ensure that individuals with ASD have the opportunities and support they need to thrive. It is our collective responsibility to understand, support, and advocate for adults with ASD.

Chapter 3: The Power of Play: Using Play Therapy to Support Children with Autism

Autism is a neurodevelopmental disorder that affects a child's social interaction, communication skills, and behavior. It is estimated that 1 in 54 children in the United States is diagnosed with autism spectrum disorder (ASD). Children with autism often face challenges in their development, including difficulties in socializing, communicating, and regulating their emotions. Play therapy has emerged as an effective intervention for children with autism, as it promotes social, emotional, and cognitive development.

Play is a fundamental aspect of childhood and is essential for the overall development of children. It provides opportunities for children to explore, learn, and develop important skills. For children with autism, play therapy offers a structured and supportive environment where they can engage in play activities that are specifically designed to address their unique needs and challenges.

Defining Play Therapy and its Benefits for Children with Autism

Play therapy is a therapeutic approach that uses play as a means of communication and expression. It is based on the understanding that play is a natural and instinctive way for children to make sense of their world and express their thoughts and feelings. The goals of play therapy for children with autism include improving communication skills, enhancing social interaction, promoting emotional regulation, and developing cognitive abilities.

One of the key benefits of play therapy for children with autism is improved communication. Many children with autism struggle with verbal communication and may have difficulty expressing themselves or understanding others. Through play therapy, children are encouraged to use various forms of communication, such as gestures, facial expressions, and body language. This helps them develop alternative means of communication and enhances their ability to understand and respond to others.

Another benefit of play therapy for children with autism is the improvement in social skills. Children with autism often struggle with social interaction and may find it challenging to initiate or maintain conversations, make eye contact, or understand social cues. Play therapy provides a safe and structured environment where children can practice social skills, such as turn-taking, sharing, and cooperation. It also helps them learn how to read social cues and understand the perspectives of others.

Emotional regulation is another area where play therapy can be beneficial for children with autism. Many children with autism have difficulty managing their emotions and may experience meltdowns or become overwhelmed in certain situations. Play therapy allows children to explore and express their emotions in a safe and supportive environment. Through play, they can learn strategies for self-regulation, such as deep breathing or using calming techniques.

The Role of Play in Developing Social and Communication Skills in Children with Autism

Play plays a crucial role in the development of social and communication skills in children with autism. It provides opportunities for children to practice and learn important social cues, such as eye contact, body language, and facial expressions. Through play, children can also develop their communication skills by using gestures, sounds, or words to express their thoughts and feelings.

One example of a play activity that promotes social and communication development is pretend play. Pretend play involves children taking on different roles and engaging in imaginary scenarios. This type of play allows children to practice social skills, such as turn-taking, sharing, and cooperation. It also encourages them to use their imagination and creativity to communicate and problem-solve.

Another example of a play activity that promotes social and communication development is board games or card games. These games require children to take turns, follow rules, and communicate with others. They provide opportunities for children to practice important social skills, such as waiting for their turn, listening to others, and expressing their thoughts or opinions.

How Play Therapy Helps Children with Autism Build Self-Esteem and Confidence

Play therapy can play a significant role in promoting self-esteem and confidence in children with autism. Many children with autism struggle with low self-esteem due to difficulties in socializing, communicating, or understanding social cues. Play therapy provides a safe and supportive environment where children can engage in activities that build their self-esteem and confidence.

One way play therapy promotes self-esteem and confidence is by allowing children to experience success and mastery. In play therapy, activities are carefully designed to match the child's abilities and interests, ensuring that they can succeed and feel a sense of accomplishment. This helps boost their self-esteem and confidence in their abilities.

Another way play therapy promotes self-esteem and confidence is by providing opportunities for children to make choices and have control over their play experiences. In play therapy, children are encouraged to make decisions, express their preferences, and take the lead in their play activities. This helps them develop a sense of autonomy and empowerment, which can positively impact their self-esteem and confidence.

The Different Types of Play Therapy Approaches for Children with Autism

There are different approaches to play therapy that can be used with children with autism. These approaches can be categorized into structured and unstructured play therapy.

Structured play therapy involves the use of specific play activities or interventions that are designed to target specific goals or skills. These activities are often guided by a therapist or caregiver who provides support, guidance, and feedback. Structured play therapy can include activities such as sensory play, art therapy, music therapy, or social skills groups.

Unstructured play therapy, on the other hand, allows children to engage in free play without specific goals or interventions. It provides a more open-ended and child-led approach to play therapy. Unstructured play therapy can include activities such as playing with toys, building blocks, engaging in imaginative play, or exploring nature.

Both structured and unstructured play therapy approaches have their benefits for children with autism. Structured play therapy provides a more focused and targeted approach to addressing specific goals or challenges. It allows therapists or caregivers to provide support and guidance in a structured environment. On the other hand, unstructured play therapy allows children to explore and express themselves freely. It encourages creativity, imagination, and self-expression.

The Importance of Tailoring Play Therapy to Meet the Unique Needs of Each Child with Autism

It is essential to tailor play therapy to meet the unique needs and interests of each child with autism. Every child with autism is different and has their own strengths, challenges, and preferences. By tailoring play therapy to meet each child's individual needs, therapists and caregivers can create a more effective and engaging therapeutic experience.

One strategy for tailoring play therapy is to incorporate the child's interests into the play activities. For example, if a child is interested in dinosaurs, the therapist or caregiver can use dinosaur toys or books during play therapy sessions. This not only captures the child's attention but also provides opportunities for learning and engagement.

Another strategy for tailoring play therapy is to consider the child's sensory preferences. Many children with autism have sensory sensitivities or preferences. Some may be sensitive to certain textures, sounds, or smells, while others may seek out sensory input. By understanding and accommodating these sensory preferences, therapists and caregivers can create a more comfortable and enjoyable play therapy experience for the child.

Strategies for Encouraging Play and Engagement in Children with Autism

Encouraging play and engagement in children with autism can sometimes be challenging. However, there are strategies that parents and caregivers can use to promote play and engagement in children with autism.

One strategy is to create a structured and predictable environment for play. Children with autism often thrive in environments that are organized, consistent, and predictable. By creating a designated play area with clear boundaries and rules, parents and caregivers can help children feel more comfortable and engaged in play.

Another strategy is to provide visual supports during play. Many children with autism are visual learners and benefit from visual cues or supports. Parents and caregivers can use visual schedules, visual prompts, or visual timers to help children understand and follow the rules or expectations of play.

Adapting play activities to meet the child's needs and interests is another effective strategy. For example, if a child has difficulty with fine motor skills, parents and caregivers can provide adapted toys or tools that are easier to manipulate. If a child has a special interest in trains, parents and caregivers can incorporate train-themed activities into play.

The Role of Parents and Caregivers in Supporting Play Therapy for Children with Autism

Parents and caregivers play a crucial role in supporting play therapy for children with autism. They are the child's primary caregivers and have a unique understanding of their child's strengths, challenges, and preferences. By actively participating in play therapy and implementing strategies at home, parents and caregivers can enhance the effectiveness of play therapy.

One important role of parents and caregivers is to provide a supportive and nurturing environment for play therapy. This includes creating a safe and comfortable space for play, setting aside dedicated time for play therapy sessions, and being actively engaged in the child's play activities.

Another role of parents and caregivers is to reinforce the skills learned in play therapy at home. This can be done by incorporating the strategies or techniques used in play therapy into everyday routines or activities. For example, if the child learned a calming technique during play therapy, parents can encourage the child to use it when they are feeling overwhelmed or anxious.

Parents and caregivers can also collaborate with the play therapist to set goals and monitor progress. By maintaining open communication with the play therapist, parents can stay informed about their child's progress in play therapy and work together to address any challenges or concerns that may arise.

The Benefits of Play Therapy for the Entire Family of a Child with Autism

Play therapy not only benefits the child with autism but also has positive effects on the entire family. It can improve family relationships, communication, and overall well-being.

One benefit of play therapy for the family is improved communication. Play therapy provides a safe and supportive environment where family members can engage in play activities together. This can help improve communication and understanding between family members, as they learn to listen, respond, and interact with each other in a playful and non-threatening way.

Play therapy can also improve family relationships by promoting bonding and connection. Engaging in play activities together allows family members to spend quality time with each other, creating opportunities for shared experiences and positive interactions. This can strengthen the parent-child relationship, as well as sibling relationships.

Furthermore, play therapy can have a positive impact on the overall well-being of the family. It provides a space for families to relax, have fun, and reduce stress. Play therapy can also help parents and caregivers develop new strategies and techniques for supporting their child with autism, which can lead to increased confidence and reduced feelings of overwhelm.

Addressing Challenges and Limitations in Using Play Therapy for Children with Autism

While play therapy is a valuable intervention for children with autism, there are some challenges and limitations that need to be addressed.

One common challenge is the difficulty in engaging children with autism in play activities. Some children with autism may have limited interests or preferences, making it challenging to find activities that capture their attention. In such cases, therapists and caregivers may need to be creative and adapt play activities to match the child's interests or sensory preferences.

Another challenge is the need for ongoing support and consistency. Play therapy is most effective when it is provided consistently over time. However, it can be challenging for parents and caregivers to maintain regular play therapy sessions at home or find qualified therapists who specialize in working with children with autism. It is important for parents and caregivers to seek out resources and support networks that can provide guidance and assistance in implementing play therapy.

The Ongoing Importance of Play Therapy in Supporting Children with Autism

In conclusion, play therapy is a valuable intervention for children with autism. It promotes social, emotional, and cognitive development and helps children with autism improve their communication skills, social interaction, and emotional regulation. Play therapy can be tailored to meet the unique needs and interests of each child with autism, and it is important for parents, caregivers, and professionals to prioritize play therapy in supporting children with autism. By understanding the importance of play and implementing strategies to support play therapy, we can help children with autism thrive and reach their full potential.

Chapter 4: Navigating the Education System: Tips for Parents of Children with Autism

Children with autism face unique challenges in the education system. Autism is a developmental disorder that affects a person's ability to communicate and interact with others. In the classroom, children with autism may struggle with social interactions, communication, and sensory sensitivities. It is important for educators and parents to understand these unique needs in order to provide the necessary support and accommodations for these children to succeed in school.

Understanding the Unique Needs of Children with Autism in the Education System

Children with autism have characteristics that can affect their learning and behavior in the classroom. They may have difficulty understanding and using language, which can make it challenging for them to follow instructions or express their needs. They may also struggle with social interactions, finding it difficult to make friends or understand social cues. Additionally, children with autism often have sensory sensitivities, which means they may be overwhelmed by certain sounds, lights, or textures in the classroom.

These challenges can make it difficult for children with autism to fully participate in the classroom and access the curriculum. They may become overwhelmed or anxious, leading to behavioral issues or meltdowns. It is important for educators to provide individualized support and accommodations to help these children succeed. This may include visual supports, such as schedules or visual cues, as well as sensory breaks or modifications to the environment.

Finding the Right School for Your Child with Autism: Factors to Consider

When choosing a school for your child with autism, there are several factors to consider. One option is a specialized school that specifically caters to children with autism. These schools often have smaller class sizes and trained staff who are experienced in working with children on the autism spectrum. Another option is a mainstream school that offers inclusive education, where children with autism are included in regular classrooms but receive additional support.

When considering a school, it is important to visit and meet with staff to get a sense of the environment and how they support children with autism. Look for schools that have a positive and inclusive culture, where all students are valued and supported. Ask about the training and experience of the staff, as well as the resources and supports available to children with autism.

The Importance of Individualized Education Plans (IEPs) for Children with Autism

An Individualized Education Plan (IEP) is a legal document that outlines the specific educational goals and accommodations for a child with a disability, such as autism. It is important for children with autism to have an IEP in place to ensure that their unique needs are being met in the classroom. The IEP is developed by a team of professionals, including parents, teachers, and other specialists, and is reviewed and updated annually.

The components of an effective IEP for children with autism may include specific goals related to communication, social skills, and behavior. It may also include accommodations and modifications to the curriculum, such as visual supports or sensory breaks. The IEP should be individualized to meet the unique needs of each child with autism and should be regularly monitored and adjusted as needed.

Navigating the IEP Process: Tips for Parents

The process of developing an IEP can be overwhelming for parents, but there are steps you can take to navigate this process successfully. Start by gathering information about your child's strengths and needs, including any assessments or evaluations that have been done. This will help you advocate for your child's needs during the IEP meeting.

Before the meeting, take some time to prepare by reviewing your child's current educational program and any previous IEPs. Think about what goals and accommodations you would like to see in the new IEP. During the meeting, be an active participant and advocate for your child's needs. Ask questions, provide input, and make sure that the goals and accommodations outlined in the IEP are appropriate for your child.

Advocating for Your Child with Autism in School: Strategies for Success

Advocating for your child with autism in school is an ongoing process that requires building positive relationships with school staff and effectively communicating your child's needs. Start by establishing open lines of communication with your child's teacher and other school staff. Share information about your child's strengths, challenges, and any strategies that have been successful in the past.

When addressing concerns or advocating for your child's needs, it is important to approach the conversation in a collaborative and respectful manner. Be specific about the issues you are concerned about and provide suggestions for how the school can support your child. Keep records of any conversations or meetings, including emails or written correspondence, to ensure that you have documentation of your efforts to advocate for your child.

Creating a Positive Learning Environment at Home for Children with Autism

Creating a positive learning environment at home is important for children with autism. Consistency and routine are key, as children with autism often thrive in structured environments. Establish a daily schedule that includes regular routines and activities. Use visual supports, such as visual schedules or timers, to help your child understand and anticipate what will happen next.

Create a designated space for learning and provide materials and resources that support your child's interests and abilities. Break tasks down into smaller steps and provide clear instructions. Celebrate your child's successes and provide positive reinforcement for their efforts.

Supporting Your Child's Social and Emotional Development in School

Social and emotional development is an important aspect of a child's overall development, including children with autism. It is important to work with school staff to support your child's social and emotional needs in the classroom. This may include providing opportunities for social interactions, such as structured play or group activities.

Collaborate with teachers to develop strategies to support your child's social skills, such as teaching them how to initiate conversations or join in group activities. Provide resources and supports, such as social stories or visual cues, to help your child understand and navigate social situations. Regularly check in with your child's teacher to monitor their progress and address any concerns.

Addressing Behavioral Challenges in the Classroom: Effective Approaches

Children with autism may face behavioral challenges in the classroom, such as meltdowns or disruptive behaviors. It is important for educators to address these challenges in a positive and supportive manner. One approach that has been found to be effective is positive behavior support, which focuses on teaching and reinforcing appropriate behaviors rather than punishing or suppressing challenging behaviors.

Strategies for addressing challenging behaviors may include providing clear expectations and rules, using visual supports to help children understand and follow instructions, and providing sensory breaks or accommodations to help children regulate their emotions. It is important for educators to work closely with parents and other professionals to develop a consistent approach to addressing behavioral challenges.

Helping Your Child with Autism Transition to New School Settings

Transitions can be challenging for children with autism, whether it is transitioning to a new school or moving from one grade level to another. It is important to prepare your child for these transitions by providing them with information and support. Talk to your child about the upcoming transition and provide visual supports, such as social stories or visual schedules, to help them understand what will happen.

Work closely with school staff to develop a transition plan that includes strategies and supports for your child. This may include providing additional support during the transition period, such as a buddy system or extra time to adjust to the new environment. Regularly check in with your child's teacher and provide ongoing support as needed.

Staying Informed and Involved in Your Child's Education: Resources for Parents of Children with Autism

Staying informed and involved in your child's education is crucial for ensuring that their unique needs are being met. There are many resources available for parents of children with autism, including websites, books, and support groups. These resources can provide information and strategies for supporting your child's learning and development.

It is also important to connect with other parents and advocacy organizations to share experiences and learn from others. Joining a support group or attending workshops or conferences can provide valuable support and resources. Additionally, stay in regular communication with your child's teacher and school staff to stay informed about their progress and any concerns that may arise.

In conclusion, children with autism face unique challenges in the education system, but with the right support and accommodations, they can thrive in school. It is important for educators and parents to understand the unique needs of children with autism and work together to provide individualized support. By advocating for your child's needs, creating a positive learning environment at home, and staying informed and involved in their education, you can help your child succeed in school and beyond. Remember to seek support and resources as needed to ensure that your child receives the best possible education.

Chapter 5: The Importance of Early Intervention for Low Functioning Autism

Low functioning autism is a complex neurodevelopmental disorder that affects individuals from a young age. It is characterized by significant impairments in social interaction, communication, and behavior. Early intervention plays a crucial role in supporting individuals with low functioning autism and maximizing their potential for growth and development. By identifying and addressing the challenges associated with this condition at an early stage, children can receive the necessary support and interventions to improve their quality of life.

Understanding Low Functioning Autism: What is it?

Low functioning autism, also known as severe autism, is a subtype of autism spectrum disorder (ASD). It is characterized by significant impairments in multiple areas of development, including social interaction, communication, and behavior. Individuals with low functioning autism often have limited verbal communication skills and may rely on alternative forms of communication, such as gestures or picture cards.

In addition to communication difficulties, individuals with low functioning autism may exhibit repetitive behaviors, restricted interests, and sensory sensitivities. They may struggle with changes in routine and have difficulty adapting to new environments or situations. These challenges can significantly impact their ability to function independently and engage in everyday activities.

Diagnosis of low functioning autism is typically made based on the presence of specific symptoms and behaviors outlined in the Diagnostic and Statistical Manual of Mental Disorders (DSM-5). A comprehensive evaluation by a team of healthcare professionals, including psychologists, speech therapists, and occupational therapists, is often necessary to make an accurate diagnosis.

Why Early Intervention is Crucial for Low Functioning Autism

Early intervention is crucial for individuals with low functioning autism because it provides them with the best opportunity for optimal development and improved outcomes. Research has shown that the brain undergoes significant development during early childhood, particularly in the first few years of life. This period of rapid brain growth presents a unique window of opportunity for intervention.

By intervening early, professionals can help shape the developing brain and provide targeted support to address the specific challenges associated with low functioning autism. Early intervention can help individuals acquire essential skills, such as communication, social interaction, and adaptive behavior, that are necessary for successful functioning in everyday life.

Furthermore, early intervention can help prevent or minimize the development of secondary issues that may arise as a result of untreated low functioning autism. These may include behavioral problems, anxiety, and difficulties with academic achievement. By addressing these challenges early on, individuals with low functioning autism can have a better chance of reaching their full potential and leading fulfilling lives.

The Benefits of Early Intervention for Low Functioning Autism

Early intervention for low functioning autism has been shown to have numerous benefits across various areas of development. These benefits extend beyond the immediate improvements seen during intervention and can have long-lasting effects throughout an individual's life.

One of the primary benefits of early intervention is improved social skills. Individuals with low functioning autism often struggle with social interaction and may have difficulty understanding social cues or engaging in reciprocal communication. Through targeted interventions, such as social skills training and peer interactions, individuals can learn and practice appropriate social behaviors, leading to improved social relationships and increased participation in social activities.

Another significant benefit of early intervention is better communication skills. Communication challenges are a hallmark of low functioning autism, and individuals may struggle to express their needs and wants effectively. Early intervention can provide individuals with alternative communication methods, such as sign language or augmentative and alternative communication (AAC) devices, to facilitate effective communication. This can greatly enhance their ability to express themselves and interact with others.

Cognitive development is another area that can be positively impacted by early intervention. Individuals with low functioning autism often experience cognitive deficits, including difficulties with attention, problem-solving, and memory. Through targeted cognitive interventions, such as structured teaching methods and visual supports, individuals can develop strategies to improve their cognitive abilities and enhance their overall learning potential.

Finally, early intervention can lead to improved adaptive behavior. Adaptive behavior refers to the skills necessary for independent functioning in everyday life, such as self-care, socialization, and problem-solving. Individuals with low functioning autism may struggle with these skills, but with early intervention, they can receive targeted support to develop and strengthen their adaptive skills. This can lead to increased independence and improved quality of life.

How Early Intervention Can Improve Social Skills in Low Functioning Autism

Social skills deficits are a common characteristic of low functioning autism. Individuals with this condition often struggle with understanding social cues, initiating and maintaining conversations, and engaging in appropriate social behaviors. Early intervention can play a crucial role in improving social skills and facilitating meaningful social interactions.

Social skills training is a key component of early intervention for low functioning autism. This type of intervention focuses on teaching individuals specific social skills and providing opportunities for practice and reinforcement. Social skills training may involve role-playing, modeling appropriate behaviors, and providing feedback and reinforcement for desired behaviors.

Family involvement is also essential in improving social skills in individuals with low functioning autism. Parents and caregivers can play an active role in supporting their child's social development by providing opportunities for social interaction, reinforcing positive behaviors, and modeling appropriate social skills. By working collaboratively with professionals, families can create a supportive environment that promotes the development of social skills.

The Role of Family in Early Intervention for Low Functioning Autism

Family support plays a critical role in the success of early intervention for individuals with low functioning autism. Families are often the primary caregivers and advocates for their children, and their involvement is crucial in ensuring that interventions are effective and sustainable.

Family-centered interventions recognize the importance of involving families in all aspects of the intervention process. This approach acknowledges that families have unique knowledge about their child's strengths, needs, and preferences and empowers them to actively participate in decision-making and goal-setting.

Collaboration between healthcare professionals and families is essential for successful early intervention. Professionals can provide families with information, resources, and strategies to support their child's development. In turn, families can provide valuable insights into their child's progress, preferences, and challenges, which can inform the intervention planning process.

How Early Intervention Can Help with Communication in Low Functioning Autism

Communication challenges are a significant aspect of low functioning autism. Individuals with this condition may have limited verbal communication skills or struggle to understand and use language effectively. Early intervention can help address these challenges and facilitate effective communication.

Communication interventions for low functioning autism may include a combination of strategies and approaches. These may include speech therapy, which focuses on improving speech production and language comprehension skills. Additionally, alternative forms of communication, such as sign language or picture-based communication systems, may be introduced to support individuals who have limited verbal abilities.

Augmentative and alternative communication (AAC) devices are another valuable tool in early intervention for low functioning autism. AAC devices can range from simple picture boards to sophisticated electronic devices that generate speech. These devices allow individuals to express themselves and communicate their needs and wants effectively. AAC devices can be customized to meet the unique needs of each individual and can greatly enhance their ability to communicate with others.

The Importance of Early Diagnosis for Low Functioning Autism

Early diagnosis is crucial for individuals with low functioning autism because it allows for early intervention and support. Recognizing the signs and symptoms of low functioning autism at an early stage can lead to timely interventions that can significantly impact an individual's development and overall quality of life.

There are several early signs that may indicate the presence of low functioning autism. These signs may include a lack of or limited eye contact, delayed or absent speech, repetitive behaviors, sensory sensitivities, and difficulties with social interaction. It is important for parents and caregivers to be aware of these signs and seek professional evaluation if they have concerns about their child's development.

The diagnostic process for low functioning autism typically involves a comprehensive evaluation by a team of healthcare professionals. This evaluation may include assessments of cognitive abilities, language skills, social interaction, and behavior. The goal is to gather information from multiple sources to make an accurate diagnosis and develop an individualized intervention plan.

Early diagnosis of low functioning autism has several benefits. It allows for early intervention, which can help address the specific challenges associated with the condition. Early intervention can also help prevent or minimize the development of secondary issues, such as behavioral problems or academic difficulties. Additionally, early diagnosis provides families with the knowledge and understanding they need to support their child effectively.

The Impact of Early Intervention on Cognitive Development in Low Functioning Autism

Cognitive deficits are common in individuals with low functioning autism. These deficits may manifest as difficulties with attention, problem-solving, memory, and abstract thinking. Early intervention can play a crucial role in supporting cognitive development and improving overall learning potential.

Cognitive interventions for low functioning autism often involve structured teaching methods and visual supports. Structured teaching methods provide individuals with a predictable and organized environment that supports their learning and reduces anxiety. Visual supports, such as visual schedules or visual cues, can help individuals understand and follow instructions, organize their thoughts, and remember important information.

Individualized interventions are essential in supporting cognitive development in individuals with low functioning autism. Each individual has unique strengths, challenges, and learning styles, and interventions should be tailored to meet their specific needs. By identifying an individual's strengths and building on them, professionals can help individuals develop strategies to compensate for their cognitive deficits and maximize their learning potential.

How Early Intervention Can Improve Adaptive Behavior in Low Functioning Autism

Adaptive behavior refers to the skills necessary for independent functioning in everyday life. Individuals with low functioning autism often struggle with adaptive behavior skills, such as self-care, socialization, and problem-solving. Early intervention can play a crucial role in improving adaptive behavior and promoting independence.

Adaptive behavior interventions for low functioning autism focus on teaching individuals the skills they need to function independently in various settings. These interventions may include teaching self-care skills, such as dressing and grooming, teaching social skills, such as turn-taking and sharing, and teaching problem-solving skills, such as identifying and implementing solutions to everyday challenges.

Functional skills training is an important component of adaptive behavior interventions. Functional skills refer to the skills necessary for independent living, such as cooking, cleaning, and managing money. By teaching individuals these practical skills, early intervention can help prepare them for adulthood and increase their chances of living independently.

The Challenges of Early Intervention for Low Functioning Autism

While early intervention is crucial for individuals with low functioning autism, there are several challenges that need to be addressed to ensure effective and accessible services.

One of the main challenges is the limited availability of resources. Early intervention services may be limited in some areas, making it difficult for families to access the support they need. This can result in delays in intervention and missed opportunities for early intervention.

Another challenge is the lack of trained professionals. Early intervention for low functioning autism requires a multidisciplinary approach involving professionals from various fields, such as psychology, speech therapy, and occupational therapy. However, there may be a shortage of professionals with expertise in low functioning autism, making it challenging to provide comprehensive and specialized interventions.

Cultural and linguistic barriers can also pose challenges to early intervention for low functioning autism. Different cultural beliefs and practices may influence how families perceive and seek help for their child's developmental challenges. Additionally, language barriers may make it difficult for families to communicate their concerns or understand the information provided by professionals.

Addressing these challenges requires a collaborative effort from policymakers, healthcare professionals, and communities. Increased awareness and funding can help expand access to early intervention services. Training programs can help increase the number of professionals with expertise in low functioning autism. Culturally sensitive and linguistically appropriate interventions can help ensure that all families have access to the support they need.

The Significance of Early Intervention for Low Functioning Autism

In conclusion, early intervention plays a crucial role in supporting individuals with low functioning autism and maximizing their potential for growth and development. By identifying and addressing the challenges associated with this condition at an early stage, children can receive the necessary support and interventions to improve their quality of life.

Early intervention offers numerous benefits across various areas of development, including improved social skills, better communication, enhanced cognitive development, and improved adaptive behavior. By targeting these areas through evidence-based interventions, individuals with low functioning autism can acquire essential skills and increase their chances of leading fulfilling lives.

However, there are challenges that need to be addressed to ensure effective and accessible early intervention services for low functioning autism. These challenges include limited resources, a shortage of trained professionals, and cultural and linguistic barriers. By working collaboratively and advocating for increased awareness and resources, we can create a brighter future for individuals with low functioning autism.

Chapter 6: From Diagnosis to Success: Stories of High Functioning Autism Triumphs

High Functioning Autism (HFA) is a term used to describe individuals on the autism spectrum who have average or above-average intelligence and language abilities. While there is no official medical diagnosis for HFA, it is often used to differentiate individuals with autism who do not have intellectual disabilities. People with HFA may exhibit a range of characteristics and traits that are unique to them.

Individuals with HFA often have difficulties with social interactions and communication. They may struggle with understanding social cues, maintaining eye contact, and engaging in reciprocal conversations. They may also have a strong preference for routines and repetitive behaviors. Additionally, individuals with HFA may experience sensory sensitivities, such as being overwhelmed by loud noises or certain textures.

Early Signs and Symptoms of High Functioning Autism

Early signs and symptoms of HFA can manifest in various ways. One of the key indicators is social and communication difficulties. Children with HFA may struggle to make eye contact, engage in reciprocal conversations, or understand nonverbal cues such as facial expressions or body language. They may also have difficulty understanding and expressing emotions.

Repetitive behaviors and routines are another common characteristic of HFA. Children with HFA may engage in repetitive movements such as hand-flapping or rocking back and forth. They may also have a strong need for sameness and become upset if their routines are disrupted.

Sensory sensitivities are also prevalent in individuals with HFA. They may be hypersensitive to certain sounds, textures, or smells, which can cause distress or discomfort. On the other hand, they may also seek out certain sensory experiences, such as spinning or jumping, to fulfill their sensory needs.

Diagnosis and Assessment of High Functioning Autism

Diagnosing HFA involves a comprehensive assessment process that takes into account various factors. The Diagnostic and Statistical Manual of Mental Disorders (DSM-5) provides diagnostic criteria for Autism Spectrum Disorder (ASD), which includes HFA. These criteria include social communication deficits, restricted and repetitive behaviors, and symptoms that are present in early childhood.

The assessment process typically involves gathering information from multiple sources, including parents, teachers, and healthcare professionals. Standardized assessment tools, such as the Autism Diagnostic Observation Schedule (ADOS) and the Autism Diagnostic Interview-Revised (ADI-R), may be used to gather additional information about the individual's behavior and development.

Early diagnosis and intervention are crucial for individuals with HFA. Early identification allows for early intervention services to be implemented, which can help improve outcomes and support the individual's development. Early intervention may include therapies such as Applied Behavior Analysis (ABA), speech therapy, occupational therapy, and social skills training.

Challenges Faced by Individuals with High Functioning Autism

Individuals with HFA often face unique challenges that can impact their daily lives and overall well-being. One of the main challenges is social isolation and difficulty making friends. Due to their difficulties with social interactions and communication, individuals with HFA may struggle to form meaningful connections with their peers. This can lead to feelings of loneliness and exclusion.

Misunderstandings and stigma surrounding autism can also pose challenges for individuals with HFA. Many people have misconceptions about autism and may make assumptions or judgments based on limited knowledge or stereotypes. This can lead to misunderstandings and discrimination, making it difficult for individuals with HFA to navigate social situations and be accepted by others.

Executive functioning difficulties are another common challenge faced by individuals with HFA. Executive functions refer to a set of cognitive processes that help individuals plan, organize, problem-solve, and regulate their behavior. Difficulties in executive functioning can make it challenging for individuals with HFA to manage their time, stay organized, and complete tasks independently.

Success Stories of Individuals with High Functioning Autism

Despite the challenges they may face, individuals with HFA have unique strengths and talents that can contribute to their success. Many individuals with HFA have achieved great things in various fields, including science, technology, arts, and entrepreneurship.

For example, Temple Grandin, a renowned animal behavior expert and advocate for autism, has made significant contributions to the field of animal science. Her unique perspective as an individual with autism has allowed her to revolutionize the livestock industry and improve animal welfare.

Another example is Dan Aykroyd, a successful actor and comedian who has openly discussed his diagnosis of Asperger's syndrome, a form of HFA. Aykroyd's comedic talent and ability to think outside the box have contributed to his successful career in the entertainment industry.

Individuals with HFA often possess exceptional attention to detail, strong problem-solving skills, and a unique way of thinking that can lead to innovative ideas and solutions. Their passion and dedication to their interests can also drive them to excel in their chosen fields.

Overcoming Social and Communication Difficulties

While social and communication difficulties may be challenging for individuals with HFA, there are strategies and interventions that can help them overcome these obstacles. Social skills training and therapy can provide individuals with HFA with the tools and strategies they need to navigate social interactions more effectively. These interventions may include teaching social cues, perspective-taking, and conversation skills.

Assistive technology and communication devices can also be beneficial for individuals with HFA. These tools can help facilitate communication and provide support in social situations. For example, individuals may use visual schedules or social stories to help them understand expectations and navigate daily routines.

Exposure therapy and desensitization techniques can be helpful for individuals with sensory sensitivities. These interventions involve gradually exposing individuals to sensory stimuli that they find challenging or overwhelming in a controlled and supportive environment. This can help reduce anxiety and increase tolerance to sensory experiences.

Achieving Academic and Professional Success

With the right support and accommodations, individuals with HFA can achieve academic and professional success. In the educational setting, accommodations such as extra time on tests, preferential seating, and visual supports can help individuals with HFA thrive. Individualized Education Programs (IEPs) and 504 plans can also provide additional support and accommodations tailored to the individual's needs.

In the workplace, accommodations such as flexible schedules, clear expectations, and a supportive work environment can help individuals with HFA succeed. Many companies are recognizing the unique strengths and talents of individuals with autism and are actively seeking to create inclusive workplaces.

Individuals with HFA may excel in careers that require attention to detail, problem-solving skills, and a strong focus on their interests. Fields such as computer programming, engineering, research, and creative arts can provide opportunities for individuals with HFA to utilize their strengths and contribute to society.

Entrepreneurship and self-employment can also be viable options for individuals with HFA. Many successful entrepreneurs have autism and have found success by leveraging their unique perspectives and talents. Being self-employed allows individuals with HFA to have more control over their work environment and schedule, which can be beneficial for managing their challenges.

Navigating Relationships and Building Connections

Building and maintaining relationships can be challenging for individuals with HFA, but it is not impossible. With support and understanding from others, individuals with HFA can develop meaningful connections in various areas of their lives.

In terms of romantic relationships and dating, individuals with HFA may benefit from social skills training that focuses on dating etiquette and communication skills. They may also find online dating platforms helpful, as they provide a more structured and predictable way of meeting potential partners.

Friendships can be fostered through shared interests and activities. Individuals with HFA may find it easier to connect with others who have similar hobbies or passions. Joining clubs, organizations, or support groups related to their interests can provide opportunities to meet like-minded individuals and form friendships.

Family relationships can also be challenging for individuals with HFA, as they may struggle with understanding and expressing emotions. Open and honest communication, along with education about autism, can help family members better understand and support the individual. Family therapy or counseling may also be beneficial in improving family dynamics and relationships.

Coping Strategies and Support for High Functioning Autism

Coping strategies and support are essential for individuals with HFA to manage their challenges and maintain their well-being. Self-care and stress management techniques can help individuals with HFA reduce anxiety and improve their overall mental health. This may include activities such as exercise, mindfulness, hobbies, or engaging in sensory activities that provide comfort.

Therapy and counseling can provide individuals with HFA with a safe space to explore their thoughts and emotions. Cognitive-behavioral therapy (CBT) can help individuals develop coping strategies for managing anxiety or challenging situations. Other therapeutic approaches, such as social skills training or occupational therapy, can also be beneficial.

Support groups and online communities can provide individuals with HFA a sense of belonging and connection. These groups allow individuals to share their experiences, seek advice, and receive support from others who understand their challenges. Online platforms also provide a safe space for individuals to connect with others without the pressure of face-to-face interactions.

The Importance of Advocacy and Awareness for High Functioning Autism

Advocacy efforts and initiatives play a crucial role in raising awareness about HFA and promoting acceptance and inclusion. By advocating for the rights and needs of individuals with HFA, we can work towards reducing stigma and creating a more inclusive society.

Raising awareness about HFA is essential in dispelling misconceptions and stereotypes surrounding autism. Education campaigns can help increase understanding among the general public, leading to greater acceptance and support for individuals with HFA.

Supporting research and funding for HFA is also vital in advancing our understanding of the condition and developing effective interventions. Research can help identify new strategies and treatments that can improve the lives of individuals with HFA and their families.

Celebrating the Triumphs of High Functioning Autism

In conclusion, individuals with High Functioning Autism have unique strengths and talents that should be celebrated. While they may face challenges in social interactions, communication, and sensory sensitivities, with the right support and accommodations, individuals with HFA can achieve academic and professional success, build meaningful relationships, and lead fulfilling lives.

It is important for society to recognize and appreciate the contributions of individuals with HFA and to provide the necessary support and accommodations to help them thrive. By advocating for their rights, raising awareness, and supporting research, we can create a more inclusive society that celebrates the triumphs of High Functioning Autism.

Chapter 7: From Misunderstood to Mainstream: How Autism Prevalence is Changing Society

Autism is a complex neurodevelopmental disorder that affects individuals in various ways. It is characterized by difficulties in social interaction, communication, and repetitive behaviors. Autism has a significant impact on individuals and society as a whole, making it crucial to understand and address this condition. By increasing awareness and promoting acceptance, we can create a more inclusive society that supports the needs of individuals with autism.

Understanding Autism: What is it and How Does it Affect People?

Autism, or Autism Spectrum Disorder (ASD), is a developmental disorder that typically appears in early childhood. It is characterized by persistent deficits in social communication and interaction, as well as restricted and repetitive patterns of behavior, interests, or activities. The diagnostic criteria for autism include impairments in social-emotional reciprocity, nonverbal communication skills, and developing, maintaining, and understanding relationships.

Individuals with autism may exhibit a range of behaviors and characteristics. They may have difficulty with social interactions, such as making eye contact, understanding social cues, or engaging in reciprocal conversations. They may also engage in repetitive behaviors or have intense interests in specific topics. Sensory sensitivities are also common among individuals with autism, where they may be hypersensitive or hyposensitive to certain stimuli.

The Rise in Autism Prevalence: Statistics and Trends

The prevalence of autism has been steadily increasing over the past few decades. According to the Centers for Disease Control and Prevention (CDC), the prevalence of autism in the United States is currently estimated to be 1 in 54 children. This represents a significant increase compared to previous years.

There are several possible reasons for the rise in autism diagnoses. One factor is increased awareness and improved diagnostic criteria, leading to more accurate identification of individuals with autism. Additionally, changes in societal attitudes towards neurodiversity have led to a greater acceptance of individuals with autism and an increased willingness to seek diagnosis and support.

The increase in autism diagnoses has significant implications for society and healthcare systems. It places a greater demand on resources and services to support individuals with autism and their families. It also highlights the need for increased research and understanding of autism to develop effective interventions and support strategies.

Challenging Stereotypes: Debunking Myths About Autism

There are many misconceptions and stereotypes surrounding autism that can be harmful to individuals with the condition. One common myth is that individuals with autism lack empathy or emotional connection. In reality, individuals with autism may experience emotions intensely but may struggle to express or interpret them in conventional ways.

Another misconception is that all individuals with autism have exceptional skills or savant abilities. While some individuals with autism may have specific talents or strengths, it is important to recognize that autism is a spectrum, and abilities vary widely among individuals.

Stereotypes and stigma can have a detrimental impact on individuals with autism, leading to social isolation, discrimination, and limited opportunities. It is crucial to promote accurate information and understanding of autism to challenge these stereotypes and create a more inclusive society.

Autism and Education: How Schools are Adapting to Support Students

Students with autism face unique challenges in traditional educational settings. They may struggle with social interactions, communication, sensory sensitivities, and executive functioning skills. However, schools are increasingly recognizing the importance of providing inclusive education for all students, including those with autism.

Schools employ various strategies and accommodations to support students with autism. These may include individualized education plans (IEPs), specialized instruction, visual supports, sensory breaks, social skills training, and peer support programs. By creating a supportive and inclusive environment, schools can help students with autism thrive academically and socially.

Inclusive education benefits not only students with autism but also their neurotypical peers. It promotes empathy, understanding, and acceptance among all students, fostering a more inclusive society from an early age.

The Workplace and Autism: Creating Inclusive Environments

Individuals with autism face unique challenges in the workplace, including difficulties with social interactions, sensory sensitivities, and executive functioning skills. However, with the right support and accommodations, individuals with autism can excel in the workplace and contribute valuable skills and perspectives.

Employers can create inclusive work environments by implementing strategies and accommodations to support employees with autism. These may include providing clear expectations and instructions, offering flexible work arrangements, creating sensory-friendly spaces, and promoting diversity and inclusion initiatives.

Creating inclusive work environments benefits not only individuals with autism but also the entire workforce. It fosters a culture of acceptance, diversity, and innovation, leading to improved productivity and employee satisfaction.

Autism and Relationships: Navigating Social Interactions

Individuals with autism often face challenges in social situations, making it difficult to form and maintain relationships. They may struggle with understanding social cues, interpreting nonverbal communication, or initiating and sustaining conversations. However, there are strategies that can help individuals with autism improve their social skills and build meaningful relationships.

Social skills training programs can provide individuals with autism with the tools and strategies they need to navigate social interactions successfully. These programs may focus on teaching skills such as active listening, perspective-taking, initiating conversations, and understanding social norms.

It is also important for society to understand and accept neurodiversity in relationships. By recognizing and valuing different communication styles and perspectives, we can create more inclusive and fulfilling relationships for individuals with autism.

The Impact of Autism on Families: Coping Strategies and Support

Families of individuals with autism face unique challenges that can have a significant impact on their emotional well-being and daily lives. They may experience stress, anxiety, isolation, financial strain, and difficulties accessing appropriate services and support.

Coping strategies are essential for families of individuals with autism. These may include seeking support from other families, joining support groups, accessing respite care, practicing self-care, and advocating for their child's needs.

Community and peer support are also crucial for families of individuals with autism. By connecting with others who share similar experiences, families can find understanding, validation, and practical advice.

Autism and Mental Health: Addressing Co-Occurring Conditions

Individuals with autism have a higher prevalence of co-occurring mental health conditions compared to the general population. These may include anxiety disorders, depression, attention-deficit/hyperactivity disorder (ADHD), and obsessive-compulsive disorder (OCD).

Addressing the mental health needs of individuals with autism requires an integrated and holistic approach. This may involve a combination of therapy, medication, behavioral interventions, and support services. It is crucial for healthcare providers to have a comprehensive understanding of autism and its associated mental health conditions to provide effective treatment and support.

Advocating for Autism: The Role of Activists and Organizations

Advocacy and activism play a vital role in promoting autism acceptance and inclusion in society. Activists and organizations work tirelessly to raise awareness, challenge stereotypes, advocate for policy changes, and improve access to services and support for individuals with autism.

There are many successful advocacy efforts and organizations dedicated to promoting autism acceptance. These include Autism Speaks, the Autism Society of America, the Autistic Self Advocacy Network (ASAN), and many others. These organizations provide resources, support networks, and platforms for individuals with autism and their families to share their stories and advocate for their rights.

Individuals and communities also have a role to play in advocating for autism rights. By educating themselves about autism, challenging stereotypes, promoting inclusion, and supporting individuals with autism in their communities, they can contribute to creating a more accepting and inclusive society.

Innovation and Autism: Technological Advances and Breakthroughs

Technology has the potential to revolutionize autism research, diagnosis, and treatment. There have been significant technological advances and breakthroughs in recent years that have improved our understanding of autism and provided new tools for intervention and support.

For example, virtual reality (VR) technology has been used to create immersive environments for social skills training. This allows individuals with autism to practice social interactions in a safe and controlled setting. Additionally, wearable devices and apps have been developed to monitor and manage sensory sensitivities, anxiety levels, and other aspects of daily life for individuals with autism.

While technology holds great promise, it is important to consider ethical considerations in its use for autism. Privacy, data security, accessibility, and the potential for overreliance on technology should be carefully considered to ensure that technological advancements are used responsibly and ethically.

The Future of Autism: Promoting Acceptance and Integration in Society

The future of autism lies in promoting acceptance and integration in society. By challenging stereotypes, debunking myths, providing support and accommodations, and fostering inclusive environments, we can create a society that values and includes individuals with autism.

Promoting acceptance and integration requires a multi-faceted approach. It involves education, awareness campaigns, policy changes, community support, and individual actions. By working together, we can create a future where individuals with autism are valued for their unique strengths and contributions.

Autism is a complex neurodevelopmental disorder that affects individuals in various ways. It is crucial to understand and address autism to create a more inclusive society that supports the needs of individuals with autism. By challenging stereotypes, promoting acceptance, providing support and accommodations, and advocating for autism rights, we can create a future where individuals with autism can thrive and reach their full potential. It is up to all of us to take action and promote autism acceptance and inclusion in our communities.

Chapter 8: The Genetics of Autism: A Comprehensive Guide for Parents and Caregivers

Autism spectrum disorder (ASD) is a complex neurodevelopmental disorder characterized by difficulties in social interaction, communication, and repetitive behaviors. It affects individuals across a wide range of abilities and can have a significant impact on their daily lives. While the exact cause of ASD is still not fully understood, research has shown that genetics plays a crucial role in its development.

The genetic basis of ASD is complex and involves a combination of genetic variations. Studies have identified numerous genes that are associated with an increased risk of developing ASD. These genes are involved in various biological processes, including brain development, synaptic function, and neuronal signaling. Understanding the role of genes in ASD is essential for gaining insights into the underlying mechanisms of the disorder and developing targeted treatments.

Understanding the Role of Genes in Autism Spectrum Disorder

Research has identified several genes that are associated with an increased risk of developing ASD. These genes are involved in various biological processes that are critical for brain development and function. For example, some genes associated with ASD play a role in synaptic function, which is essential for communication between neurons. Others are involved in neuronal signaling pathways or regulate gene expression during brain development.

One example of a gene associated with ASD is called SHANK3. Mutations in this gene have been found in individuals with

Phelan-McDermid syndrome, a rare genetic disorder characterized by intellectual disability and ASD. SHANK3 is involved in the formation and function of synapses, which are the connections between neurons. Mutations in this gene can disrupt synaptic function and lead to the characteristic features of ASD.

Another gene associated with ASD is called PTEN. Mutations in this gene have been found in individuals with PTEN hamartoma tumor syndrome, a condition that increases the risk of developing certain types of tumors as well as ASD and other neurodevelopmental disorders. PTEN is involved in regulating cell growth and division, as well as neuronal signaling pathways. Mutations in this gene can disrupt these processes and contribute to the development of ASD.

Genetic Testing for Autism: What You Need to Know

Genetic testing can provide valuable information about the genetic basis of ASD. There are several different types of genetic tests that can be used to identify genetic variations associated with ASD. These tests include chromosomal microarray analysis, whole exome sequencing, and targeted gene panel testing.

Chromosomal microarray analysis is a test that can detect large-scale chromosomal abnormalities, such as deletions or duplications of genetic material. This test is particularly useful for identifying genetic variations that are associated with syndromic forms of ASD, where individuals have additional physical or intellectual features in addition to ASD.

Whole exome sequencing is a test that can analyze the protein-coding regions of the genome, which are known as exons. This test can identify small-scale genetic variations, such as single nucleotide variants or small insertions or deletions. Whole exome sequencing is particularly useful for identifying rare genetic variants that may be associated with an increased risk of developing ASD.

Targeted gene panel testing is a test that focuses on specific genes that are known to be associated with ASD. This test can provide targeted information about genetic variations in these genes and is particularly useful when there is a strong suspicion of a specific genetic cause for ASD.

While genetic testing can provide valuable information about the genetic basis of ASD, it also has limitations. Not all individuals with ASD will have identifiable genetic variations, and even when genetic variations are identified, their significance may not always be clear. Genetic testing also cannot predict the severity or specific features of ASD in an individual. Therefore, it is important to interpret the results of genetic testing in the context of other clinical information and to seek guidance from healthcare professionals who specialize in genetics.

Types of Genetic Mutations Associated with Autism

There are several different types of genetic mutations that can cause ASD. These mutations can occur in various genes and can have different effects on brain development and function. Some of the most common types of genetic mutations associated with ASD include:

1. Deletions and Duplications: These mutations involve the loss or gain of genetic material. Deletions and duplications can disrupt the normal functioning of genes and can lead to changes in brain development and function.

2. Single Nucleotide Variants: These mutations involve changes in a single nucleotide, or DNA building block, within a gene. Single nucleotide variants can alter the function of a gene and can contribute to the development of ASD.

3. Copy Number Variants: These mutations involve changes in the number of copies of a particular gene or genes. Copy number variants can disrupt the normal balance of gene expression and can lead to changes in brain development and function.

4. Gene Regulatory Mutations: These mutations involve changes in the regulatory regions of genes, which control when and where genes are expressed. Gene regulatory mutations can alter the expression of genes involved in brain development and function and can contribute to the development of ASD.

The Importance of Family History in Autism Diagnosis

Family history can provide important clues for ASD diagnosis and management. Research has shown that individuals with a family history of ASD are at an increased risk of developing the disorder themselves. The risk is higher for individuals who have a first-degree relative, such as a sibling or parent, with ASD.

Studying family history can help identify patterns of inheritance and provide insights into the genetic basis of ASD. For example, if multiple individuals in a family have ASD, it suggests that there may be a genetic cause for the disorder. Understanding the genetic implications of having a family member with ASD can help guide genetic testing and inform treatment decisions.

In addition to genetic factors, family history can also provide information about environmental factors that may contribute to the development of ASD. For example, if multiple individuals in a family have ASD and were exposed to a common environmental factor, such as a medication or toxin, it suggests that the environmental factor may play a role in the development of the disorder.

Genetics and Environmental Factors in Autism Development

The development of ASD is influenced by a combination of genetic and environmental factors. While genetics plays a significant role in the development of ASD, it is not the sole determinant. Environmental factors can interact with genetic variations to increase or decrease the risk of developing ASD.

Research has shown that certain environmental factors, such as maternal infections during pregnancy or exposure to certain medications or toxins, can increase the risk of developing ASD in individuals who have a genetic predisposition. These environmental factors can interact with genetic variations to disrupt normal brain development and function.

The interaction between genetics and environmental factors in the development of ASD is complex and not fully understood. However, research is ongoing to better understand how these factors interact and to identify specific environmental factors that may contribute to the development of ASD.

Genetic Counseling for Families Affected by Autism

Genetic counseling is an important service for families affected by ASD. Genetic counselors are healthcare professionals who specialize in genetics and can provide information and support to individuals and families who are at risk of or affected by genetic conditions, including ASD.

Genetic counseling for families affected by ASD typically involves a comprehensive evaluation of family history, genetic testing options, and interpretation of test results. Genetic counselors can help families understand the genetic basis of ASD, including the potential inheritance patterns and recurrence risks.

Genetic counselors can also provide guidance on family planning options for individuals or couples who are at risk of having a child with ASD. This may include discussing reproductive options, such as prenatal testing or preimplantation genetic diagnosis, which can help identify genetic variations associated with ASD before or during pregnancy.

Current Research on the Genetics of Autism

Research on the genetics of ASD is advancing our understanding of the disorder and informing new treatments. Recent studies have identified numerous genes associated with an increased risk of developing ASD, providing insights into the biological processes that are disrupted in individuals with the disorder.

One area of research that is particularly promising is the identification of genetic subtypes of ASD. Researchers have found that individuals with ASD can have different combinations of genetic variations, which may contribute to differences in symptoms and treatment responses. Understanding these genetic subtypes can help guide personalized treatment approaches and improve outcomes for individuals with ASD.

Another area of research that is advancing our understanding of ASD is the study of gene-environment interactions. Researchers are investigating how genetic variations interact with environmental factors to increase or decrease the risk of developing ASD. This research may lead to the identification of specific environmental factors that can be targeted for prevention or treatment strategies.

Genetic Treatments for Autism: Current State and Future Directions

While there are currently no specific genetic treatments for ASD, research is ongoing to develop targeted therapies based on the underlying genetic causes of the disorder. One approach being explored is gene therapy, which involves delivering a functional copy of a mutated gene or modifying the expression of a gene to restore normal function.

Another approach being investigated is pharmacogenomics, which involves using genetic information to guide medication selection and dosing. By understanding an individual's genetic variations, healthcare providers can identify medications that are more likely to be effective and minimize the risk of adverse reactions.

In addition to these targeted therapies, there is also a focus on developing interventions that can improve outcomes for individuals with ASD regardless of their specific genetic variations. These interventions may include behavioral therapies, educational interventions, and support services that can help individuals with ASD develop skills and reach their full potential.

Supporting Individuals with Autism and Their Families through Genetic Testing

Healthcare providers play a crucial role in supporting individuals with ASD and their families through the genetic testing process. It is important for healthcare providers to provide accurate and up-to-date information about genetic testing options, benefits, and limitations.

In addition to providing information, healthcare providers should also offer emotional support and resources for families affected by ASD. A diagnosis of ASD can be overwhelming for families, and it is important to provide a safe and supportive environment where they can ask questions, express concerns, and access appropriate resources.

Healthcare providers should also collaborate with other professionals, such as genetic counselors, psychologists, and educators, to ensure that individuals with ASD receive comprehensive care that addresses their unique needs. This may include developing personalized treatment plans, coordinating therapies and interventions, and advocating for appropriate educational services.

Navigating the Genetics of Autism as a Parent or Caregiver

Navigating the genetics of ASD as a parent or caregiver can be challenging, but it is important to remember that you are not alone. There are resources available to support you through the diagnostic process and beyond.

Seeking out support groups or organizations that specialize in ASD can provide valuable information, guidance, and emotional support. These groups can connect you with other families who have similar experiences and can offer insights into navigating the genetics of ASD.

It is also important to work closely with healthcare providers who specialize in genetics and ASD. They can provide accurate information about genetic testing options, interpret test results, and guide treatment decisions based on your child's specific needs.

Remember that every individual with ASD is unique, and there is no one-size-fits-all approach to diagnosis or treatment. By seeking out support and resources, you can empower yourself to make informed decisions and provide the best possible care for your child.

Chapter 9: Breaking Down Barriers: The Latest Autism Research Findings

Autism Spectrum Disorder (ASD) is a neurodevelopmental disorder that affects social interaction, communication, and behavior. It is characterized by a range of symptoms and severity levels, which is why it is referred to as a "spectrum" disorder. The prevalence of ASD has been steadily increasing over the years, with current estimates suggesting that 1 in 54 children in the United States are diagnosed with ASD.

Common characteristics of ASD include difficulties in social interaction and communication, repetitive behaviors and restricted interests, and sensory sensitivities. Individuals with ASD may have difficulty understanding and responding to social cues, making eye contact, and engaging in reciprocal conversation. They may also engage in repetitive behaviors such as hand-flapping or rocking, and have intense interests in specific topics.

Early Detection and Diagnosis of Autism Spectrum Disorder

Early detection and diagnosis of ASD is crucial for providing appropriate interventions and support. Research has shown that early intervention can significantly improve outcomes for individuals with ASD. Therefore, it is important for parents, caregivers, and healthcare professionals to be aware of the signs and symptoms of ASD.

Signs and symptoms of ASD can vary widely from person to person, but some common red flags include delayed or absent speech, lack of social engagement or interest in others, repetitive behaviors or movements, and sensory sensitivities. If these signs are present, it is important to seek a comprehensive evaluation from a healthcare professional who specializes in diagnosing ASD.

Screening and diagnostic tools are used to assess the presence of ASD. The Modified Checklist for Autism in Toddlers (M-CHAT) is a commonly used screening tool for children between the ages of 16-30 months. If a child screens positive on the M-CHAT, further evaluation is recommended using diagnostic tools such as the Autism Diagnostic Observation Schedule (ADOS) or the Autism Diagnostic Interview-Revised (ADI-R).

Genetics and Autism: What the Latest Research Tells Us

Genetic factors play a significant role in the development of ASD. Studies have shown that there is a strong genetic component to ASD, with heritability estimates ranging from 50-90%. However, the genetics of ASD are complex and involve a combination of genetic variations.

Current research on genetic causes of ASD has identified several genes and genetic mutations that are associated with an increased risk of developing ASD. These genes are involved in various biological processes, including brain development, synaptic function, and neuronal signaling. However, it is important to note that these genetic variations are not the sole cause of ASD and that other factors, such as environmental influences, also play a role.

The implications of genetic research in ASD are twofold. First, it provides valuable insights into the underlying biological mechanisms of ASD, which can help inform the development of targeted treatments and interventions. Second, it highlights the importance of early detection and diagnosis, as genetic testing can provide valuable information about an individual's risk for developing ASD and guide personalized interventions.

Environmental Factors and Autism: Debunking Common Myths

There are many misconceptions about the role of environmental factors in the development of ASD. It is important to debunk these myths and understand the current research on environmental influences on ASD.

One common misconception is that vaccines cause autism. However, numerous studies have shown that there is no link between vaccines and the development of ASD. The original study that suggested a link between vaccines and autism has been thoroughly discredited and retracted.

Current research on environmental factors and ASD suggests that there may be some prenatal and early life exposures that increase the risk of developing ASD. These include maternal infections during pregnancy, exposure to certain medications or chemicals, and advanced parental age. However, it is important to note that these factors are not causative but rather increase the risk of developing ASD.

Understanding the role of environment in ASD is important for several reasons. First, it helps to dispel myths and misconceptions that can lead to stigma and discrimination against individuals with ASD. Second, it highlights the importance of creating supportive and inclusive environments for individuals with ASD. Finally, it provides valuable information for prevention efforts and interventions.

The Role of Brain Development in Autism Spectrum Disorder

Brain development plays a critical role in the development of ASD. Research has shown that there are differences in brain structure and function in individuals with ASD compared to typically developing individuals.

In typical children, brain development follows a predictable pattern, with different regions of the brain maturing at different rates. However, in children with ASD, there are differences in the timing and trajectory of brain development. These differences can affect various aspects of brain function, including social cognition, language processing, and sensory integration.

Understanding the differences in brain development in ASD is important for developing targeted interventions and treatments. For example, interventions that focus on improving social skills may target specific areas of the brain involved in social cognition. Similarly, interventions that address sensory sensitivities may target areas of the brain involved in sensory processing.

Sensory Processing Differences in Autism: What We Know So Far

Sensory processing differences are common in individuals with ASD. Many individuals with ASD have heightened sensitivity to sensory stimuli or may seek out sensory stimulation. This can manifest as hypersensitivity to sounds, lights, or textures, or as a need for repetitive or intense sensory experiences.

Current research on sensory processing in ASD has identified several underlying mechanisms that contribute to these differences. For example, studies have shown that individuals with ASD may have differences in the way their brains process and integrate sensory information. They may also have differences in the way they regulate their arousal levels and attention.

Understanding sensory processing differences in ASD is important for developing effective interventions and accommodations. For example, individuals with hypersensitivity to certain sounds may benefit from noise-canceling headphones or a quiet space to retreat to. Similarly, individuals who seek out sensory stimulation may benefit from sensory integration therapy or the use of sensory tools such as fidget toys.

Communication Challenges in Autism Spectrum Disorder

Communication challenges are a hallmark feature of ASD. Many individuals with ASD have difficulty with both verbal and nonverbal communication. They may have delayed or absent speech, difficulty initiating or maintaining conversations, and challenges understanding and using nonverbal cues such as gestures or facial expressions.

Current research on communication in ASD has identified several underlying factors that contribute to these challenges. For example, studies have shown that individuals with ASD may have differences in the way their brains process and interpret language. They may also have difficulties with social cognition, which can affect their ability to understand and respond to social cues.

Understanding the communication challenges in ASD is important for developing effective interventions and supports. For example, individuals with limited verbal communication skills may benefit from alternative communication systems such as sign language or augmentative and alternative communication (AAC) devices. Similarly, interventions that focus on improving social skills and understanding social cues can help individuals with ASD navigate social interactions more effectively.

Social Skills and Autism: Breaking Down Barriers

Social skills challenges are another common feature of ASD. Many individuals with ASD have difficulty understanding and navigating social interactions. They may struggle with making friends, interpreting social cues, and understanding social norms.

Current research on social skills in ASD has identified several underlying factors that contribute to these challenges. For example, studies have shown that individuals with ASD may have differences in the way their brains process and interpret social information. They may also have difficulties with theory of mind, which is the ability to understand and attribute mental states to oneself and others.

Understanding the social skills challenges in ASD is important for developing effective interventions and supports. For example, interventions that focus on teaching social skills can help individuals with ASD learn how to initiate conversations, make eye contact, and interpret social cues. Similarly, interventions that focus on promoting inclusion and acceptance can help break down barriers and create more inclusive communities for individuals with ASD.

Behavioral Interventions and Autism: What Works Best?

Behavioral interventions are a cornerstone of treatment for ASD. These interventions focus on teaching new skills and reducing challenging behaviors. There are several evidence-based practices for behavioral interventions in ASD.

Applied Behavior Analysis (ABA) is one of the most widely used and well-researched behavioral interventions for ASD. ABA focuses on breaking down skills into smaller, manageable steps and using positive reinforcement to teach new skills. It can be used to target a wide range of skills, including communication, social skills, and daily living skills.

Other evidence-based practices for behavioral interventions in ASD include Social Skills Training, Cognitive Behavioral Therapy (CBT), and Parent Training. These interventions focus on teaching specific skills and strategies to individuals with ASD and their families.

It is important to note that behavioral interventions should be individualized to meet the unique needs of each individual with ASD. A comprehensive assessment should be conducted to identify the specific strengths and challenges of the individual, and interventions should be tailored to address these specific needs.

Medication and Autism: Current Research and Controversies

Medication is sometimes used as a treatment option for individuals with ASD, particularly when there are co-occurring conditions such as ADHD or anxiety. However, the use of medication in ASD is a topic of ongoing research and controversy.

There is currently no medication that specifically targets the core symptoms of ASD. However, there are medications that can help manage some of the associated symptoms, such as hyperactivity or aggression. These medications are typically prescribed on an individual basis, taking into account the specific needs and challenges of the individual.

The use of medication in ASD is controversial due to concerns about potential side effects and long-term effects on brain development. Some studies have suggested that certain medications may be associated with an increased risk of adverse effects, such as weight gain or metabolic changes. However, more research is needed to fully understand the risks and benefits of medication use in ASD.

It is important for individuals with ASD and their families to work closely with healthcare professionals to weigh the potential benefits and risks of medication use. A comprehensive treatment plan should take into account the individual's unique needs and challenges, and should include a combination of behavioral interventions, educational supports, and other therapies.

Looking Ahead: Promising Areas of Autism Research for the Future

There are several promising areas of research in ASD that hold potential for improving our understanding and treatment of the disorder. One area of research is the development of biomarkers for early detection and diagnosis. Biomarkers are measurable indicators that can help identify individuals at risk for developing ASD or track the progress of interventions.

Another area of research is the development of targeted interventions based on individual characteristics. Research has shown that there is significant heterogeneity within the ASD population, with different individuals having different strengths and challenges. Developing interventions that are tailored to the specific needs of each individual can lead to more effective outcomes.

Finally, there is ongoing research on the role of the gut microbiome in ASD. The gut microbiome refers to the trillions of bacteria that live in our digestive system and play a crucial role in our health. Emerging research suggests that there may be a link between the gut microbiome and ASD, and that targeting the gut microbiome may have therapeutic potential.

Conclusion:

In conclusion, Autism Spectrum Disorder is a complex neurodevelopmental disorder that affects social interaction, communication, and behavior. Early detection and diagnosis are crucial for providing appropriate interventions and support. Genetic factors play a significant role in the development of ASD, and current research is shedding light on the underlying genetic causes. Environmental factors also play a role in ASD, although there are many misconceptions about their impact. Understanding brain development, sensory processing, communication, and social skills in ASD is important for developing effective interventions and supports. Behavioral interventions are a cornerstone of treatment for ASD, and there are several evidence-based practices available. The use of medication in ASD is a topic of ongoing research and controversy. Looking ahead, there are several promising areas of research that hold potential for improving our understanding and treatment of ASD. Continued research and understanding of ASD is crucial for providing the best possible support and interventions for individuals with ASD and their families.

Chapter 10: Unraveling the Mystery: The Top 5 Causes of Autism

Autism Spectrum Disorder (ASD) is a neurodevelopmental disorder characterized by persistent deficits in social communication and interaction, as well as restricted and repetitive patterns of behavior, interests, or activities. It is a complex disorder that affects individuals differently, with a wide range of symptoms and severity levels. ASD is typically diagnosed in early childhood, although some individuals may not receive a diagnosis until later in life.

The prevalence of ASD has been steadily increasing over the past few decades. According to the Centers for Disease Control and Prevention (CDC), approximately 1 in 54 children in the United States have been diagnosed with ASD. This represents a significant increase from previous estimates, highlighting the need for further research into the causes and risk factors associated with the disorder.

Genetic Factors and Autism

Genetic factors play a significant role in the development of Autism Spectrum Disorder. Studies have shown that there is a strong genetic component to ASD, with heritability estimates ranging from 50% to 90%. This means that genetics can account for a significant portion of the risk for developing ASD.

There are several common genetic mutations associated with Autism Spectrum Disorder. One of the most well-known is a mutation in the gene called SHANK3, which is involved in the development and function of synapses in the brain. Mutations in other genes, such as FMR1, MECP2, and PTEN, have also been linked to ASD. These mutations can disrupt normal brain development and function, leading to the characteristic symptoms of ASD.

Environmental Factors and Autism

In addition to genetic factors, environmental factors may also contribute to the development of Autism Spectrum Disorder. Environmental factors refer to any external influences that can impact an individual's risk for developing ASD. These factors can include prenatal exposures, such as maternal infections or exposure to certain medications, as well as postnatal exposures, such as exposure to toxins or pollutants.

There is growing evidence to suggest that certain environmental factors may increase the risk of developing ASD. For example, maternal exposure to air pollution during pregnancy has been associated with an increased risk of ASD in offspring. Other studies have found a link between prenatal exposure to certain chemicals, such as pesticides or flame retardants, and an increased risk of ASD. However, it is important to note that these environmental factors are not the sole cause of ASD and likely interact with genetic factors to contribute to the development of the disorder.

Prenatal and Perinatal Factors and Autism

Prenatal and perinatal factors refer to events or conditions that occur during pregnancy or around the time of birth that may increase the risk of developing Autism Spectrum Disorder. These factors can include maternal health conditions, such as gestational diabetes or preeclampsia, as well as complications during labor and delivery, such as prematurity or low birth weight.

Research has shown that certain prenatal and perinatal factors may be associated with an increased risk of ASD. For example, maternal infections during pregnancy, such as rubella or cytomegalovirus, have been linked to an increased risk of ASD in offspring. Other studies have found an association between preterm birth and an increased risk of ASD. However, it is important to note that not all individuals who experience these prenatal and perinatal factors will develop ASD, highlighting the complex interplay between genetic and environmental factors in the development of the disorder.

Neurological Factors and Autism

Neurological factors play a crucial role in Autism Spectrum Disorder. The brains of individuals with ASD often show differences in structure and function compared to typically developing individuals. These differences can affect various areas of the brain involved in social communication, sensory processing, and executive functioning.

One example of a neurological factor associated with ASD is abnormal connectivity between different brain regions. Studies using neuroimaging techniques, such as functional magnetic resonance imaging (fMRI), have shown that individuals with ASD may have altered patterns of connectivity in the brain. This disrupted connectivity can impact the integration of information and the coordination of brain activity, leading to the social and behavioral difficulties observed in ASD.

Immunological Factors and Autism

Immunological factors refer to the immune system's role in the development of Autism Spectrum Disorder. There is evidence to suggest that immune dysregulation may contribute to the development of ASD. The immune system plays a crucial role in protecting the body against infections and maintaining overall health. However, when the immune system becomes dysregulated, it can lead to inflammation and other immune-related abnormalities that may impact brain development and function.

Several immunological factors have been implicated in ASD. For example, studies have found elevated levels of certain cytokines, which are signaling molecules involved in immune responses, in individuals with ASD. Other studies have found an association between maternal immune activation during pregnancy and an increased risk of ASD in offspring. However, more research is needed to fully understand the complex relationship between the immune system and ASD.

The Role of Epigenetics in Autism

Epigenetics refers to changes in gene expression that do not involve changes to the underlying DNA sequence. These changes can be influenced by various factors, including environmental exposures and lifestyle choices. Epigenetic modifications can alter gene expression patterns and contribute to the development of Autism Spectrum Disorder.

There is growing evidence to suggest that epigenetic factors may play a role in the development of ASD. For example, studies have found differences in DNA methylation patterns, which is one type of epigenetic modification, in individuals with ASD compared to typically developing individuals. Other studies have found an association between prenatal exposure to certain chemicals, such as bisphenol A (BPA) or phthalates, and changes in DNA methylation patterns in offspring.

Gastrointestinal Factors and Autism

Gastrointestinal (GI) factors refer to the role of the digestive system in Autism Spectrum Disorder. Many individuals with ASD also experience gastrointestinal symptoms, such as abdominal pain, constipation, or diarrhea. These GI symptoms may be related to underlying gut dysbiosis, which refers to an imbalance in the gut microbiota.

Research has shown that individuals with ASD may have alterations in the composition and diversity of their gut microbiota compared to typically developing individuals. These alterations can impact the production of certain metabolites and neurotransmitters, which can in turn affect brain development and function. However, more research is needed to fully understand the complex relationship between the gut microbiota and ASD.

Nutritional Deficiencies and Autism

Nutritional deficiencies refer to inadequate intake or absorption of essential nutrients that are necessary for proper growth and development. There is evidence to suggest that certain nutritional deficiencies may be associated with an increased risk of Autism Spectrum Disorder.

For example, studies have found an association between low levels of certain vitamins, such as vitamin D or folate, during pregnancy and an increased risk of ASD in offspring. Other studies have found an association between deficiencies in certain minerals, such as zinc or magnesium, and an increased risk of ASD. However, it is important to note that nutritional deficiencies are not the sole cause of ASD and likely interact with other factors to contribute to the development of the disorder.

Psychological Factors and Autism

Psychological factors refer to the role of mental processes and behaviors in Autism Spectrum Disorder. Individuals with ASD often experience difficulties with social communication and interaction, as well as restricted and repetitive patterns of behavior. These psychological factors can impact various aspects of daily life, including relationships, education, and employment.

There is evidence to suggest that certain psychological factors may contribute to the development and maintenance of ASD symptoms. For example, individuals with ASD may have difficulties with theory of mind, which refers to the ability to understand and attribute mental states to oneself and others. Other psychological factors, such as executive functioning deficits or sensory processing difficulties, may also contribute to the challenges experienced by individuals with ASD.

Conclusion and Future Directions in Autism Research

In conclusion, Autism Spectrum Disorder is a complex neurodevelopmental disorder that is influenced by a variety of factors. Genetic factors play a significant role in the development of ASD, with several common genetic mutations associated with the disorder. Environmental factors, such as prenatal exposures or postnatal toxins, may also contribute to the risk of developing ASD. Prenatal and perinatal factors, neurological factors, immunological factors, epigenetic factors, gastrointestinal factors, nutritional deficiencies, and psychological factors all play a role in the development and manifestation of ASD.

Future directions in Autism Spectrum Disorder research should focus on further understanding the complex interplay between these various factors. This will involve conducting large-scale studies that incorporate multiple levels of analysis, including genetics, epigenetics, neuroimaging, and environmental exposures. By gaining a better understanding of the underlying causes and risk factors associated with ASD, researchers can develop more targeted interventions and treatments for individuals with the disorder.

Chapter 11: Breaking Down Barriers with Autism Resources: Accessible Support for All

Autism is a complex neurodevelopmental disorder that affects millions of individuals worldwide. It is characterized by difficulties in social interaction, communication, and repetitive behaviors. For individuals with autism and their families, accessing appropriate resources and support is crucial for their overall well-being and quality of life. Autism resources encompass a wide range of services, therapies, and support systems that aim to help individuals with autism reach their full potential and lead fulfilling lives. In this article, we will explore the importance of autism resources, the barriers to accessing them, the different types of resources available, and strategies for navigating the resource landscape.

Understanding the Importance of Autism Resources

Autism resources play a vital role in the lives of individuals with autism and their families. These resources provide support, guidance, and tools to help individuals with autism navigate the challenges they face on a daily basis. They also offer valuable information and education to parents and caregivers, empowering them to better understand and meet the unique needs of their loved ones.

One of the key reasons why autism resources are crucial is that they help individuals with autism develop essential skills and abilities. Many individuals with autism struggle with social interaction and communication, which can make it difficult for them to form meaningful relationships and participate fully in society. Autism resources such as therapy and social skills training can provide individuals with the tools they need to improve their social interactions and communication skills, enabling them to build relationships and engage more effectively with others.

In addition to skill development, autism resources also play a significant role in improving the overall quality of life for individuals with autism and their families. These resources can help individuals with autism manage their sensory sensitivities, develop coping strategies for anxiety or meltdowns, and enhance their independence in daily activities. For families, autism resources can provide much-needed support, guidance, and respite care, reducing stress levels and improving overall family functioning.

Overcoming Barriers to Accessing Autism Support

While autism resources are essential, many individuals and families face barriers when trying to access them. Some common barriers include lack of awareness about available resources, financial constraints, geographical limitations, and long waiting lists for services. These barriers can prevent individuals with autism from receiving the support they need in a timely manner, leading to delays in intervention and potential negative outcomes.

To overcome these barriers, it is crucial to increase awareness about available autism resources and ensure that information is easily accessible to individuals and families. This can be done through community outreach programs, educational campaigns, and partnerships with healthcare providers and schools. Additionally, efforts should be made to make autism resources more affordable and accessible to all individuals and families, regardless of their financial situation or geographical location. This can be achieved through government funding, subsidies, and the expansion of telehealth services.

Key Types of Autism Resources Available

There are various types of autism resources available to individuals with autism and their families. These resources can be broadly categorized into therapy, education, and support groups.

Therapy is a crucial component of autism support. It includes interventions such as Applied Behavior Analysis (ABA), speech therapy, occupational therapy, and sensory integration therapy. These therapies aim to address specific challenges faced by individuals with autism, such as communication difficulties, sensory sensitivities, and behavioral issues. Therapy sessions are typically conducted by trained professionals who work closely with individuals with autism to develop personalized goals and strategies for improvement.

Education is another key aspect of autism resources. It includes specialized educational programs that cater to the unique learning needs of individuals with autism. These programs may be provided in mainstream schools with additional support or in specialized schools that focus specifically on serving students with autism. The goal of these programs is to provide a structured and supportive learning environment that promotes academic growth, social skills development, and independence.

Support groups are also valuable resources for individuals with autism and their families. These groups provide a safe and supportive space for individuals with autism to connect with others who share similar experiences. They offer opportunities for social interaction, skill-building, and emotional support. Support groups can be in-person or online, and they may focus on specific topics such as parenting, self-advocacy, or sibling support.

Navigating the Autism Resource Landscape

Navigating the autism resource landscape can be overwhelming for individuals and families, especially when faced with a new diagnosis or when seeking additional support. However, there are strategies that can help make the process easier and more manageable.

One important tip is to start by gathering information about available resources in your local community. This can be done by reaching out to healthcare providers, schools, and autism organizations. These sources can provide valuable information about therapy providers, educational programs, and support groups in your area.

Networking and building a support system is also crucial when navigating the autism resource landscape. Connecting with other parents and individuals with autism can provide valuable insights, recommendations, and emotional support. Online forums, social media groups, and local support groups are great places to connect with others who are going through similar experiences.

It is also important to be proactive in advocating for your needs and the needs of your loved ones. This may involve reaching out to healthcare providers or school administrators to request specific services or accommodations. It may also involve advocating for increased accessibility and funding for autism resources at a broader level by contacting local representatives or participating in advocacy organizations.

The Role of Technology in Autism Support

Technology has revolutionized the way we access information and connect with others, and it has also had a significant impact on autism support. Technology can be used to enhance communication skills, provide virtual therapy sessions, offer educational resources, and facilitate social interaction.

One way technology is used in autism support is through the use of communication apps and devices. These tools can help individuals with autism improve their communication skills by providing visual supports, augmentative and alternative communication (AAC) systems, and social stories. They can also facilitate social interaction by providing virtual platforms for individuals with autism to connect with others.

Virtual therapy sessions have also become increasingly popular, especially in situations where in-person therapy is not feasible or accessible. Telehealth services allow individuals with autism to receive therapy sessions from the comfort of their own homes, reducing barriers such as transportation and geographical limitations. These virtual sessions can be conducted through video calls, allowing therapists to provide guidance, support, and interventions remotely.

There are also numerous online resources and educational platforms that offer a wealth of information and tools for individuals with autism and their families. These resources can include educational videos, interactive games, social skills training modules, and behavior management strategies. They can be accessed at any time and from anywhere, providing flexibility and convenience for individuals and families.

Advocating for Increased Autism Resource Accessibility

Advocacy plays a crucial role in ensuring that autism resources are accessible to all individuals who need them. Advocacy efforts can help raise awareness about the importance of autism support, promote understanding and acceptance of individuals with autism, and push for increased funding and accessibility of resources.

One important strategy for advocating for increased accessibility is to get involved in local and national autism organizations. These organizations often have advocacy committees or initiatives that work towards improving policies, funding, and services for individuals with autism. By joining these organizations or participating in their advocacy efforts, individuals and families can have a direct impact on shaping the future of autism resources.

Another strategy is to reach out to local representatives and policymakers to voice concerns and advocate for change. This can be done through letters, emails, phone calls, or in-person meetings. Sharing personal stories and experiences can be particularly impactful in raising awareness and generating support for increased accessibility to autism resources.

It is also important to engage with the media to promote accurate portrayals of individuals with autism and to challenge misconceptions and stereotypes. By sharing personal stories, participating in interviews, or writing articles, individuals and families can help shape public perception and increase understanding of autism.

How to Create an Individualized Autism Support Plan

Creating an individualized support plan is essential for individuals with autism as it helps identify their unique needs and goals and outlines the strategies and resources required to meet those needs. An individualized support plan should be comprehensive, person-centered, and flexible to accommodate changes and progress over time.

One important step in creating an individualized support plan is to conduct a thorough assessment of the individual's strengths, challenges, and goals. This can be done through evaluations conducted by healthcare professionals, educators, and therapists. The assessment should consider various domains such as communication, social skills, behavior management, sensory sensitivities, and academic abilities.

Based on the assessment results, specific goals can be identified for each domain. These goals should be realistic, measurable, and tailored to the individual's unique needs. For example, a goal may be to improve communication skills by increasing vocabulary or using alternative communication methods such as sign language or AAC devices.

Once the goals are established, strategies and resources can be identified to help achieve those goals. This may include therapy sessions, educational programs, support groups, assistive technology devices, and community resources. It is important to consider the individual's preferences, strengths, and interests when selecting these resources to ensure they are engaging and meaningful.

Regular monitoring and evaluation of the individual's progress is also crucial in an individualized support plan. This allows for adjustments to be made as needed and ensures that the plan remains relevant and effective over time.

The Benefits of Early Intervention for Autism

Early intervention refers to the provision of services and support for individuals with autism at a young age, typically before the age of three. Research has consistently shown that early intervention can have a significant positive impact on the development and outcomes of individuals with autism.

Early intervention focuses on addressing the core deficits of autism, such as communication, social interaction, and behavior management, during a critical period of brain development. By providing targeted interventions and therapies at an early age, individuals with autism have a greater chance of acquiring essential skills and abilities that will benefit them throughout their lives.

One of the key benefits of early intervention is improved communication skills. Early intervention programs often include speech therapy and other communication-focused interventions that help individuals with autism develop language skills, improve nonverbal communication, and enhance social interaction. These skills are crucial for building relationships, participating in school and community activities, and achieving independence.

Early intervention also plays a significant role in reducing challenging behaviors commonly associated with autism. By providing behavior management strategies and teaching individuals with autism alternative ways to communicate their needs and emotions, early intervention can help reduce frustration, anxiety, and meltdowns. This leads to improved emotional well-being and overall quality of life for individuals with autism and their families.

Finding Affordable Autism Resources for Families

Accessing affordable autism resources is a common concern for many families. The cost of therapy sessions, educational programs, and specialized equipment can be a significant financial burden for families already facing various challenges associated with autism.

However, there are strategies that families can employ to find affordable autism resources. One important tip is to explore government-funded programs and services. Many countries have government initiatives that provide funding or subsidies for therapy sessions, educational programs, and assistive technology devices. These programs may have specific eligibility criteria, so it is important to research and understand the requirements.

Another strategy is to reach out to local nonprofit organizations that provide support for individuals with autism. These organizations often offer scholarships or financial assistance programs that can help offset the costs of therapy or educational programs. Additionally, they may have partnerships or collaborations with service providers that offer discounted rates for their members.

It is also worth exploring community resources and support groups that offer free or low-cost services. These resources may include parent support groups, community centers, or recreational programs that cater to individuals with autism. While they may not provide specialized therapy or educational services, they can still offer valuable support, social interaction, and skill-building opportunities.

Addressing Stigma and Misconceptions About Autism

Stigma and misconceptions surrounding autism can have a significant impact on the lives of individuals with autism and their families. It can lead to social isolation, discrimination, and limited access to resources and opportunities. Addressing stigma and promoting understanding is crucial for creating an inclusive society that embraces and supports individuals with autism.

One strategy for addressing stigma is through education and awareness campaigns. These campaigns can provide accurate information about autism, debunk common myths and misconceptions, and promote acceptance and understanding. They can be targeted at schools, workplaces, healthcare providers, and the general public to ensure a widespread impact.

Another strategy is to promote positive portrayals of individuals with autism in the media. By showcasing the talents, strengths, and achievements of individuals with autism, the media can challenge stereotypes and promote a more accurate understanding of autism. This can be done through documentaries, news stories, interviews, or fictional representations in movies or TV shows.

It is also important to encourage inclusive practices in schools, workplaces, and community settings. This includes providing accommodations and support for individuals with autism to fully participate in activities and events. It also involves fostering a culture of acceptance and respect where individuals with autism are valued for their unique contributions.

The Future of Autism Resources: Innovations and Trends

The field of autism resources is constantly evolving, driven by advancements in technology, research findings, and changing societal attitudes towards autism. Several emerging trends and innovations hold promise for improving the accessibility and effectiveness of autism resources.

One emerging trend is the use of virtual reality (VR) technology in therapy and skill-building programs. VR can provide immersive and interactive experiences that simulate real-life situations, allowing individuals with autism to practice social skills, navigate sensory challenges, and develop coping strategies in a controlled and safe environment. This technology has the potential to enhance therapy outcomes and provide more personalized interventions.

Another trend is the integration of assistive technology devices into everyday life. Assistive technology devices such as wearable sensors, communication apps, and smart home systems can help individuals with autism manage their sensory sensitivities, improve communication, and enhance independence. These devices are becoming more affordable and accessible, making them valuable tools for individuals with autism and their families.

Research into the genetic and neurobiological underpinnings of autism is also advancing our understanding of the disorder and paving the way for targeted interventions. As our knowledge of the biological mechanisms behind autism grows, it is likely that we will see the development of more personalized and effective therapies that address the specific needs of individuals with autism.

Autism resources are crucial for individuals with autism and their families to lead fulfilling lives and reach their full potential. These resources provide support, guidance, and tools to help individuals with autism navigate the challenges they face on a daily basis. They also play a significant role in improving overall quality of life for individuals with autism and their families.

However, accessing autism resources can be challenging due to various barriers such as lack of awareness, financial constraints, and geographical limitations. Strategies for overcoming these barriers include increasing awareness about available resources, making resources more affordable and accessible, and advocating for change at the systemic level. Increasing awareness about available resources can be done through public education campaigns, community outreach programs, and partnerships with schools and healthcare providers. This can help individuals with autism and their families understand what resources are available to them and how to access them. Financial constraints can be a significant barrier for many individuals and families seeking autism resources. To make resources more affordable, governments and organizations can provide subsidies or grants to cover the costs of assessments, therapies, and support services. Additionally, insurance companies can be encouraged to provide comprehensive coverage for autism-related treatments. Geographical limitations can make it difficult for individuals in rural or remote areas to access autism resources. To address this barrier, telehealth services can be expanded to provide remote assessments, consultations, and therapy sessions. Mobile clinics or outreach programs can also be established to bring resources directly to underserved communities. Advocating for change at the systemic level is crucial for overcoming these barriers in the long term. This includes pushing for policy changes that prioritize autism resources and support services, as well as advocating for increased funding for research and intervention programs. Collaboration between government agencies, healthcare providers, educators, and advocacy groups is essential to ensure that individuals with autism have equal access to the resources they need to thrive.

Chapter 12: Breaking the Stigma: How Autism Support is Changing Lives

Autism is a neurodevelopmental disorder that affects individuals in various ways. It is characterized by difficulties in social interaction, communication, and repetitive behaviors. According to the Centers for Disease Control and Prevention (CDC), autism affects approximately 1 in 54 children in the United States. It is important to understand and support individuals with autism because they have unique strengths and abilities that can contribute to society. By providing the necessary support and resources, we can help individuals with autism reach their full potential and lead fulfilling lives.

Understanding the Misconceptions: The Truth about Autism

There are many misconceptions surrounding autism that can lead to misunderstandings and stigma. One common misconception is that individuals with autism lack intelligence or are not capable of learning. However, this is far from the truth. While individuals with autism may have challenges in certain areas, they also have unique strengths and abilities. Many individuals with autism have exceptional memory skills, attention to detail, and a strong focus on their interests.

Another misconception is that autism is caused by bad parenting or vaccines. However, extensive research has shown that neither of these factors causes autism. Autism is a complex disorder with a strong genetic component. It is important to dispel these myths and provide accurate information about autism to promote understanding and acceptance.

The Importance of Early Intervention: How It Can Change Lives

Early intervention refers to the support and services provided to children with autism from birth to age three. Research has shown that early diagnosis and intervention can greatly improve outcomes for children with autism. Early intervention programs focus on developing communication, social, and cognitive skills through various therapies such as speech therapy, occupational therapy, and applied behavior analysis (ABA).

One example of a successful early intervention program is the Early Start Denver Model (ESDM). This program combines behavioral therapy with play-based activities to promote social interaction, communication, and cognitive development in young children with autism. Studies have shown that children who receive early intervention using the ESDM approach have better language and cognitive skills, as well as improved social interaction compared to those who do not receive early intervention.

The Role of Autism Support in Empowering Individuals with Autism

Autism support refers to the various services and resources available to individuals with autism and their families. These supports can range from educational programs and therapies to community resources and advocacy groups. The goal of autism support is to help individuals with autism reach their full potential and lead independent and fulfilling lives.

There are different types of autism support available, depending on the needs of the individual. For children with autism, educational support is crucial. This can include specialized schools or inclusive education programs that provide individualized instruction and support. Therapies such as speech therapy, occupational therapy, and ABA are also important in helping individuals with autism develop essential skills.

In addition to educational and therapeutic support, community resources play a vital role in empowering individuals with autism. These resources can include social skills groups, recreational programs, and vocational training programs. By providing a supportive environment and opportunities for social interaction and skill development, individuals with autism can gain confidence and independence.

The Challenges of Raising a Child with Autism: Strategies for Coping

Raising a child with autism can present unique challenges for families. One common challenge is the difficulty in communication and social interaction. Children with autism may have limited verbal skills or struggle to understand social cues, which can make it challenging for them to express their needs or form relationships with others.

Another challenge is managing challenging behaviors. Individuals with autism may engage in repetitive behaviors or have difficulty regulating their emotions, which can lead to meltdowns or other disruptive behaviors. This can be stressful for both the child and their family members.

Coping strategies for families include seeking support from professionals such as therapists or counselors who specialize in working with individuals with autism. These professionals can provide guidance and strategies for managing challenging behaviors and improving communication skills. It is also important for families to take care of their own well-being by seeking respite care or joining support groups where they can connect with other families facing similar challenges.

The Benefits of Inclusive Education for Children with Autism

Inclusive education refers to the practice of including students with disabilities, including autism, in general education classrooms alongside their typically developing peers. Inclusive education has many benefits for children with autism. It promotes social interaction and peer relationships, which can help improve communication and social skills. It also provides opportunities for children with autism to learn from their peers and develop a sense of belonging.

One example of a successful inclusive education program is the Peer-Mediated Instruction and Intervention (PMII) model. This model involves training typically developing peers to provide support and instruction to students with autism in the classroom. Research has shown that students with autism who participate in PMII programs have improved social skills, academic performance, and overall well-being.

The Impact of Technology on Autism Support: Innovative Solutions for Everyday Challenges

Technology has had a significant impact on autism support, providing innovative solutions for everyday challenges faced by individuals with autism. For example, communication apps and devices have been developed to help individuals with limited verbal skills communicate their needs and wants. These apps use pictures or symbols that individuals can select to express themselves.

Another area where technology has made a difference is in the field of virtual reality (VR). VR technology can be used to create virtual environments that simulate real-life situations, allowing individuals with autism to practice social skills in a safe and controlled setting. This can be particularly helpful for individuals who struggle with social interactions or have difficulty generalizing skills learned in therapy to real-life situations.

The Power of Community Support: Building a Strong Network for Families with Autism

Community support plays a crucial role in empowering families with autism. It provides a sense of belonging and connection, as well as access to resources and information. Community support can come in various forms, such as support groups, parent networks, and community events.

Support groups provide a safe space for families to share their experiences, seek advice, and connect with others who understand the challenges they face. Parent networks can also be valuable in providing information about local resources and services, as well as advocating for the needs of individuals with autism in the community.

Community events that are inclusive and autism-friendly can also help families feel supported and included. These events provide opportunities for individuals with autism to participate in activities and socialize with others in a supportive environment.

The Role of Occupational Therapy in Supporting Individuals with Autism

Occupational therapy (OT) plays a vital role in supporting individuals with autism by helping them develop the skills necessary for daily living and independence. OT focuses on improving fine motor skills, sensory processing, self-care skills, and social skills.

One example of a successful occupational therapy program is the Sensory Integration Therapy (SIT). This therapy uses sensory experiences to help individuals with autism regulate their sensory responses and improve their ability to process sensory information. By addressing sensory challenges, individuals with autism can better engage in daily activities and participate in their environment.

The Need for Increased Awareness and Advocacy for Autism Support

Raising awareness about autism is crucial in promoting understanding and acceptance. It helps dispel misconceptions and reduce stigma surrounding autism. Increased awareness can also lead to improved access to support and resources for individuals with autism and their families.

Advocacy plays a vital role in improving autism support by advocating for policies and legislation that promote inclusion, accessibility, and equal opportunities for individuals with autism. Advocacy efforts can also focus on increasing funding for research, services, and supports for individuals with autism.

The Benefits of Employment Opportunities for Individuals with Autism

Employment opportunities are essential for individuals with autism to lead independent and fulfilling lives. Many individuals with autism have unique strengths and abilities that can be valuable in the workplace. However, they often face barriers to employment, such as difficulty with social interactions or sensory sensitivities.

There are successful employment programs that focus on providing job training and support for individuals with autism. These programs match individuals with autism to jobs that align with their strengths and interests, and provide ongoing support and accommodations in the workplace. By creating inclusive work environments and providing the necessary support, individuals with autism can thrive in their careers.

Celebrating Diversity: Embracing Differences and Breaking the Stigma Surrounding Autism

It is important to celebrate diversity and embrace differences when it comes to autism. Each individual with autism is unique, with their own strengths, abilities, and challenges. By embracing these differences, we can create a more inclusive society that values and respects individuals with autism.

Breaking the stigma surrounding autism is crucial in promoting acceptance and understanding. Stigma can lead to discrimination and exclusion, preventing individuals with autism from fully participating in society. By challenging stereotypes and promoting positive narratives about autism, we can create a more inclusive and accepting society for all.

Understanding and supporting individuals with autism is essential in promoting their well-being and helping them reach their full potential.

By dispelling misconceptions, providing early intervention, offering autism support, embracing diversity, and advocating for increased awareness and resources, we can create a more inclusive society that values and supports individuals with autism. It is our collective responsibility to break the stigma surrounding autism and ensure that individuals with autism have equal opportunities to thrive in all aspects of life.

Chapter 13: Beyond the Basics: Advanced Autism Therapies for Enhanced Learning and Development

Autism is a neurodevelopmental disorder that affects individuals in various ways, impacting their social skills, communication abilities, and behavior. It is estimated that 1 in 54 children in the United States is diagnosed with autism, making it one of the most prevalent developmental disorders. The impact of autism extends beyond the individual diagnosed; it affects families, caregivers, and communities as well.

Early intervention and therapy are crucial for individuals with autism to help them reach their full potential. Research has shown that early intervention can lead to significant improvements in behavior, communication, and social skills. Advanced autism therapies go beyond traditional approaches and provide innovative techniques and interventions to address the unique needs of individuals with autism.

Applied Behavior Analysis (ABA) Therapy: An Effective Approach for Autism Treatment

Applied Behavior Analysis (ABA) therapy is a widely recognized and evidence-based approach for treating autism. ABA therapy focuses on understanding and modifying behavior through the application of behavioral principles. The goal of ABA therapy is to increase desired behaviors and decrease challenging behaviors.

ABA therapy utilizes various techniques such as positive reinforcement, prompting, shaping, and fading to improve behavior, communication, and social skills. For example, a therapist may use discrete trial training to teach a child with autism how to respond to specific cues or prompts. This technique breaks down complex skills into smaller steps and provides immediate reinforcement for correct responses.

Research has consistently shown the effectiveness of ABA therapy in improving behavior, communication, and social skills in individuals with autism. Studies have demonstrated that ABA therapy can lead to significant improvements in language development, adaptive skills, and academic performance. It is important to note that ABA therapy is highly individualized and tailored to meet the specific needs of each individual with autism.

Occupational Therapy: Enhancing Fine Motor Skills and Sensory Integration

Occupational therapy plays a crucial role in supporting individuals with autism in developing and improving their fine motor skills and sensory integration. Occupational therapists work with individuals to help them engage in meaningful activities and develop the skills necessary for daily living.

Fine motor skills, such as writing, cutting, and buttoning, are essential for individuals with autism to participate in school, work, and leisure activities. Occupational therapists use various interventions, such as hand strengthening exercises, sensory play, and adaptive equipment, to improve fine motor skills.

Sensory integration is another area that occupational therapy addresses. Many individuals with autism have sensory processing issues, where they may be over or under-sensitive to certain sensory stimuli. Occupational therapists use sensory integration techniques to help individuals regulate their responses to sensory input and improve their ability to engage in daily activities.

Speech Therapy: Improving Communication and Language Skills

Communication and language skills are often a significant challenge for individuals with autism. Speech therapy focuses on improving communication abilities by targeting speech production, language comprehension, and social communication skills.

Speech therapists use a variety of techniques and interventions to address the unique needs of individuals with autism. For example, they may use visual supports, such as picture schedules or communication boards, to enhance understanding and expression. They may also incorporate social stories or role-playing activities to improve social communication skills.

The goal of speech therapy is to help individuals with autism effectively communicate their wants, needs, and thoughts. Research has shown that speech therapy can lead to significant improvements in language development, articulation, and social communication skills in individuals with autism.

Social Skills Training: Enhancing Social Interaction and Emotional Regulation

Social interaction and emotional regulation are areas of difficulty for many individuals with autism. Social skills training focuses on teaching individuals with autism the necessary skills to interact with others effectively and regulate their emotions.

Social skills training involves teaching individuals how to initiate conversations, maintain eye contact, take turns, and understand nonverbal cues. It also includes teaching strategies for managing emotions, such as deep breathing or using a calming strategy.

The goal of social skills training is to help individuals with autism develop meaningful relationships, navigate social situations, and regulate their emotions effectively. Research has shown that social skills training can lead to improvements in social interaction, emotional regulation, and overall quality of life for individuals with autism.

Cognitive Behavioral Therapy (CBT): Addressing Anxiety and Challenging Behaviors

Anxiety and challenging behaviors are common among individuals with autism. Cognitive Behavioral Therapy (CBT) is a therapeutic approach that focuses on identifying and modifying negative thoughts and behaviors.

CBT helps individuals with autism understand the connection between their thoughts, feelings, and behaviors. It teaches them strategies to challenge negative thoughts and replace them with more positive and adaptive ones. CBT also helps individuals develop coping skills to manage anxiety and challenging behaviors.

CBT can be particularly beneficial for individuals with autism who experience anxiety or engage in self-injurious or aggressive behaviors. Research has shown that CBT can lead to significant reductions in anxiety symptoms and challenging bring behaviors in individuals with autism.

Music Therapy: A Creative Approach for Autism Treatment

Music therapy is a creative approach that uses music to address the unique needs of individuals with autism. Music therapists use various techniques, such as singing, playing instruments, and movement, to engage individuals in therapeutic activities.

Music therapy can help individuals with autism improve their communication skills, social interaction, emotional expression, and sensory integration. For example, singing songs with repetitive lyrics can help individuals improve their language skills and memory. Playing instruments can enhance fine motor skills and coordination.

Music therapy provides a non-threatening and enjoyable environment for individuals with autism to express themselves and engage in meaningful activities. Research has shown that music therapy can lead to improvements in communication, social interaction, and emotional well-being in individuals with autism.

Animal-Assisted Therapy: Enhancing Emotional Well-being and Social Skills

Animal-assisted therapy involves the use of animals, such as dogs or horses, to enhance emotional well-being and social skills in individuals with autism. Animals can provide a calming and non-judgmental presence, which can help individuals with autism feel more comfortable and engaged.

Animal-assisted therapy can help individuals with autism develop empathy, improve social skills, and reduce anxiety. For example, interacting with a therapy dog can help individuals practice social interaction and emotional regulation. Taking care of an animal can also teach responsibility and improve self-esteem.

Research has shown that animal-assisted therapy can lead to improvements in emotional well-being, social skills, and overall quality of life for individuals with autism. It is important to note that animal-assisted therapy should be conducted under the guidance of trained professionals to ensure the safety and well-being of both the individual with autism and the animal.

Sensory Integration Therapy: Addressing Sensory Processing Issues

Sensory integration therapy focuses on addressing sensory processing issues in individuals with autism. Many individuals with autism have difficulty processing sensory information, which can lead to sensory overload or sensory-seeking behaviors.

Sensory integration therapy involves providing individuals with opportunities to engage in sensory-rich activities that help them regulate their responses to sensory input. For example, therapists may use swings, trampolines, or weighted blankets to provide deep pressure input and promote relaxation.

The goal of sensory integration therapy is to help individuals with autism better understand and respond to sensory input in their environment. Research has shown that sensory integration therapy can lead to improvements in sensory processing, self-regulation, and overall functioning in individuals with autism.

Assistive Technology: Enhancing Learning and Communication

Assistive technology refers to devices or tools that help individuals with autism enhance their learning and communication abilities.

Assistive technology can range from simple tools like visual schedules or communication boards to more complex devices like speech-generating devices or tablets.

Assistive technology can help individuals with autism overcome communication barriers and participate more fully in their environment. For example, a speech-generating device can help individuals who have limited verbal abilities communicate their wants and needs. Visual schedules can provide structure and support for individuals with autism to navigate daily routines.

The goal of assistive technology is to provide individuals with the tools they need to communicate effectively, access information, and participate in activities. Research has shown that assistive technology can lead to improvements in communication, academic performance, and independence in individuals with autism.

The Importance of Advanced Autism Therapies for Enhanced Learning and Development

In conclusion, advanced autism therapies play a crucial role in supporting the learning and development of individuals with autism. Each therapy approach discussed in this article offers unique techniques and interventions to address the specific needs of individuals with autism.

It is important for families and caregivers to seek out advanced autism therapies early on to provide individuals with the best chance for success. Individualized therapy plans that incorporate a combination of different therapies can help individuals with autism reach their full potential and lead fulfilling lives.

By understanding the importance of advanced autism therapies and advocating for their availability and accessibility, we can ensure that individuals with autism receive the support they need to thrive.

Chapter 14: Beyond Medication: Alternative Approaches to Autism Treatment

Autism is a neurodevelopmental disorder that affects millions of people worldwide. Traditionally, the approach to treating autism has focused on medication as the primary form of intervention. However, medication may not always be the best option for treating autism, as it often comes with side effects and may not address the underlying causes of the disorder. In recent years, there has been a growing recognition of the importance of alternative therapies and treatments for individuals with autism. These alternative approaches focus on addressing the core symptoms of autism and improving overall quality of life.

Behavioral Therapy

Behavioral therapy is a widely recognized and effective approach to treating autism. It focuses on modifying behaviors and teaching new skills to individuals with autism. The goal of behavioral therapy is to help individuals with autism develop more adaptive behaviors and improve their overall functioning.

There are several techniques used in behavioral therapy for autism. One such technique is Applied Behavior Analysis (ABA), which involves breaking down complex behaviors into smaller, manageable steps and providing positive reinforcement for desired behaviors. Another technique is Social Skills Training, which focuses on teaching individuals with autism how to interact with others and navigate social situations. Additionally, Cognitive Behavioral Therapy (CBT) can be used to help individuals with autism identify and change negative thought patterns and behaviors.

Nutritional Therapy

Diet can play a significant role in the symptoms experienced by individuals with autism. Many parents and caregivers have reported improvements in behavior, communication, and overall functioning when dietary changes are made. Some common dietary changes that may benefit individuals with autism include eliminating gluten and casein from the diet, increasing intake of omega-3 fatty acids, and reducing consumption of processed foods and artificial additives.

Gluten-free and casein-free diets have gained popularity in the autism community due to anecdotal reports of improvements in behavior and communication. Gluten is a protein found in wheat, barley, and rye, while casein is a protein found in dairy products. Some individuals with autism may have sensitivities or allergies to these proteins, which can exacerbate their symptoms. Omega-3 fatty acids, found in fish oil and flaxseed oil, have been shown to have anti-inflammatory properties and may help reduce inflammation in the brain, potentially improving symptoms of autism. Additionally, reducing the consumption of processed foods and artificial additives can help support overall health and well-being.

Sensory Integration Therapy

Sensory integration therapy is a form of therapy that focuses on helping individuals with autism process and respond to sensory information more effectively. Many individuals with autism have sensory processing difficulties, meaning they may be over or under-sensitive to certain sensory stimuli. Sensory integration therapy aims to help individuals with autism develop more appropriate responses to sensory input.

There are several techniques used in sensory integration therapy for autism. One such technique is deep pressure therapy, which involves applying firm pressure to the body through activities such as weighted blankets or compression garments. This can help individuals with autism feel more grounded and regulated. Another technique is sensory diets, which involve providing a structured schedule of sensory activities throughout the day to help individuals with autism regulate their sensory systems. Additionally, sensory integration therapy may involve activities such as swinging, bouncing on a therapy ball, or engaging in tactile play to help individuals with autism develop better sensory processing skills.

Music Therapy

Music therapy has been shown to be a highly effective intervention for individuals with autism. Music has a unique ability to engage and stimulate the brain, making it an ideal tool for improving communication and social skills in individuals with autism.

Music therapy techniques for autism can include singing songs, playing musical instruments, and engaging in rhythmic activities. These activities can help individuals with autism develop better communication skills by encouraging them to use their voices and engage in verbal and nonverbal communication. Music therapy can also help improve social skills by providing opportunities for group interaction and collaboration. Additionally, music therapy can help individuals with autism regulate their emotions and reduce anxiety, as music has a calming and soothing effect on the brain.

Animal-Assisted Therapy

Animal-assisted therapy involves the use of animals to help individuals with autism improve their emotional regulation and overall well-being. Animals have a unique ability to provide comfort and support, making them ideal companions for individuals with autism.

Animal-assisted therapy techniques for autism can include activities such as petting and grooming animals, walking or playing with animals, and engaging in structured activities with animals. These activities can help individuals with autism develop better emotional regulation skills by providing a source of comfort and companionship. Animals can also help individuals with autism improve their social skills by providing opportunities for interaction and connection. Additionally, animal-assisted therapy can help individuals with autism develop empathy and compassion, as they learn to care for and interact with animals.

Art Therapy

Art therapy is a form of therapy that uses art materials and creative expression to help individuals with autism improve their emotional well-being and overall functioning. Art has a unique ability to engage the brain and provide a means of self-expression for individuals with autism.

Art therapy techniques for autism can include activities such as drawing, painting, sculpting, and collage-making. These activities can help individuals with autism express their thoughts, feelings, and experiences in a nonverbal way. Art therapy can also help individuals with autism develop better self-awareness and self-esteem by providing a safe space for exploration and self-expression. Additionally, art therapy can help individuals with autism develop better fine motor skills and coordination through engaging in art-making activities.

Yoga and Mindfulness

Yoga and mindfulness practices have been shown to be highly beneficial for individuals with autism. These calming practices can help individuals with autism regulate their emotions, reduce anxiety, and improve overall well-being.

Yoga techniques for autism can include activities such as yoga poses, breathing exercises, and relaxation techniques. These activities can help individuals with autism develop better body awareness and coordination. Mindfulness techniques for autism can include activities such as meditation, deep breathing, and guided imagery. These activities can help individuals with autism develop better self-regulation skills and reduce stress and anxiety.

Chiropractic Care

Chiropractic care is a form of alternative medicine that focuses on the diagnosis and treatment of musculoskeletal disorders, particularly those affecting the spine. While there is limited research on the use of chiropractic care for autism, some parents and caregivers have reported improvements in behavior, communication, and overall functioning after receiving chiropractic adjustments.

Chiropractic techniques for autism can include spinal adjustments, massage therapy, and physical therapy exercises. These techniques aim to improve spinal alignment and reduce tension in the muscles and joints. Some individuals with autism may have misalignments or subluxations in their spine, which can affect their overall health and well-being. Chiropractic care can help address these misalignments and promote better nervous system function.

Acupuncture

Acupuncture is an ancient Chinese medical practice that involves the insertion of thin needles into specific points on the body to promote healing and balance. While there is limited research on the use of acupuncture for autism, some parents and caregivers have reported improvements in behavior, communication, and overall functioning after receiving acupuncture treatments.

Acupuncture techniques for autism can include the insertion of needles into specific points on the body, as well as the use of other modalities such as acupressure or laser therapy. These techniques aim to stimulate the body's natural healing response and promote balance in the body's energy systems. Some individuals with autism may have imbalances or blockages in their energy systems, which can affect their overall health and well-being. Acupuncture can help address these imbalances and promote better physical and emotional health.

In conclusion, it is important to consider alternative approaches to autism treatment, as medication may not always be the best option. There are a variety of alternative therapies and treatments available that can help individuals with autism improve their symptoms and overall quality of life. These therapies focus on addressing the core symptoms of autism and promoting overall well-being. By exploring different therapies and treatments, individuals with autism and their loved ones can find the best approach for their unique needs.

Chapter 15: The Power of Inclusion: Supporting Individuals with Autism

Autism, also known as Autism Spectrum Disorder (ASD), is a neurodevelopmental disorder that affects communication, social interaction, and behavior. It is characterized by difficulties in social interaction, repetitive patterns of behavior, and restricted interests. Autism is a lifelong condition that affects individuals differently, with a wide range of abilities and challenges.

Inclusion refers to the practice of ensuring that individuals with Autism are fully integrated into society and have equal access to education, employment, and community participation. Inclusion is important because it promotes acceptance, understanding, and equal opportunities for individuals with Autism. It allows them to develop their skills, reach their full potential, and lead fulfilling lives.

This blog post aims to explore the benefits of inclusion for individuals with Autism, strategies for overcoming barriers to inclusion, creating a supportive environment in education and employment settings, promoting social interaction and communication, accommodating sensory sensitivities, involving families and caregivers in promoting inclusion, advocating for community support and resources, addressing mental health needs, building self-esteem and confidence, and the future of Autism support.

The Benefits of Inclusion for Individuals with Autism

Inclusion has numerous benefits for individuals with Autism. Firstly, it improves social skills. By being included in mainstream settings such as schools and workplaces, individuals with Autism have more opportunities to interact with their peers and develop their social skills. They learn how to communicate effectively, make friends, and navigate social situations. This not only enhances their quality of life but also prepares them for future relationships and employment.

Secondly, inclusion increases self-esteem and confidence. When individuals with Autism are included in mainstream settings and given the opportunity to succeed alongside their peers, they develop a sense of belonging and self-worth. They gain confidence in their abilities and feel valued for who they are. This positive self-image translates into improved mental health and overall well-being.

Thirdly, inclusion leads to better academic and employment outcomes. When individuals with Autism are included in mainstream education and given appropriate support, they have the opportunity to learn and thrive academically. They can access the same curriculum as their peers and receive individualized accommodations to meet their unique needs. This sets them up for success in higher education and future employment. In the workplace, inclusion allows individuals with Autism to contribute their unique skills and perspectives, leading to increased productivity and job satisfaction.

Lastly, inclusion reduces anxiety and depression. When individuals with Autism are included in mainstream settings, they experience a sense of acceptance and belonging. This reduces feelings of isolation and loneliness, which are common among individuals with Autism. By being included, they also have access to support systems that can help them manage their anxiety and depression effectively.

Overcoming Barriers to Inclusion: Common Misconceptions and Stereotypes

Inclusion for individuals with Autism is often hindered by myths and stereotypes surrounding the condition. One common misconception is that individuals with Autism are intellectually disabled. In reality, Autism does not affect intelligence, and many individuals with Autism have average or above-average IQs. This misconception can lead to low expectations and limited opportunities for individuals with Autism.

Another stereotype is that individuals with Autism lack empathy or emotional connection. While it is true that some individuals with Autism may struggle with understanding and expressing emotions, this does not mean they lack empathy. In fact, many individuals with Autism have a deep capacity for empathy and care deeply about others.

These misconceptions and stereotypes can have a significant impact on inclusion for individuals with Autism. They can lead to discrimination, exclusion, and limited opportunities for education, employment, and community participation. To overcome these barriers, it is important to educate society about the true nature of Autism and challenge these misconceptions through awareness campaigns, training programs, and advocacy efforts.

Strategies for overcoming these barriers include promoting positive portrayals of individuals with Autism in the media, providing education and training to teachers, employers, and community members, and creating inclusive policies and practices that ensure equal opportunities for individuals with Autism.

Creating a Supportive Environment: Strategies for Inclusive Education and Employment

Creating a supportive environment is crucial for promoting inclusion in education and employment settings. In the classroom, accommodations can be made to meet the unique needs of individuals with Autism. These accommodations may include visual supports, such as schedules and visual cues, sensory breaks, preferential seating, and individualized instruction. It is also important to provide training and support to teachers to help them understand and meet the needs of students with Autism.

In the workplace, accommodations can be made to ensure that individuals with Autism can perform their job duties effectively. These accommodations may include flexible work schedules, clear communication strategies, task breakdowns, and sensory-friendly workspaces. Employers can also provide training and support to supervisors and colleagues to promote understanding and acceptance of individuals with Autism.

Individualized support plans are essential for promoting inclusion in both education and employment settings. These plans outline the specific accommodations and supports that an individual with Autism requires to succeed. They are developed collaboratively between the individual, their family or caregiver, educators or employers, and any other relevant professionals. Individualized support plans ensure that the unique needs of individuals with Autism are met and that they have equal access to education and employment opportunities.

Strategies for promoting inclusion in education and employment settings include fostering a culture of acceptance and understanding, providing ongoing training and support to educators and employers, creating opportunities for peer support and mentorship, and celebrating the strengths and accomplishments of individuals with Autism.

Supporting Social Interaction and Communication: Techniques for Effective Interaction

Promoting social interaction and communication is essential for inclusion. Individuals with Autism may struggle with social skills such as initiating conversations, maintaining eye contact, understanding nonverbal cues, and taking turns in conversation. However, with the right support and strategies, they can develop these skills and engage in meaningful social interactions.

Strategies for promoting social interaction and communication include providing explicit instruction in social skills, using visual supports to facilitate understanding, creating structured opportunities for social interaction, and promoting peer support and mentorship. It is also important to create a safe and supportive environment where individuals with Autism feel comfortable expressing themselves and taking risks in social situations.

Understanding nonverbal communication is crucial for effective interaction with individuals with Autism. Many individuals with Autism may have difficulty understanding and using nonverbal cues such as facial expressions, body language, and tone of voice. It is important to be patient, use clear and direct language, and provide visual supports to enhance understanding. It is also helpful to use visual supports such as social stories or visual schedules to prepare individuals with Autism for social situations and help them navigate them successfully.

Sensory Sensitivities and Accommodations: Promoting Comfort and Productivity

Individuals with Autism often have sensory sensitivities, which means they may be hypersensitive or hyposensitive to certain sensory stimuli. They may be overwhelmed by loud noises, bright lights, strong smells, or certain textures. These sensory sensitivities can significantly impact their comfort and productivity in the classroom or workplace.

Accommodations for sensory sensitivities can include providing a quiet space for breaks or relaxation, using noise-canceling headphones or earplugs, adjusting lighting levels, providing access to sensory tools such as fidget toys or weighted blankets, and allowing for flexible seating options. It is important to consult with the individual with Autism to understand their specific sensory needs and preferences.

Strategies for promoting productivity and comfort include creating a sensory-friendly environment that minimizes sensory distractions, providing opportunities for movement breaks or physical activity, incorporating sensory activities into the daily routine, and allowing individuals with Autism to self-regulate their sensory experiences.

The Role of Families and Caregivers in Promoting Inclusion

Families and caregivers play a crucial role in promoting inclusion for individuals with Autism. They are often the primary advocates and support systems for individuals with Autism, and their involvement can greatly impact their success.

Family and caregiver support is important because it provides individuals with Autism with a strong foundation of love, acceptance, and understanding. Families and caregivers can provide emotional support, help individuals with Autism navigate social situations, advocate for their needs, and connect them with resources and services.

Strategies for promoting inclusion at home include creating a structured and predictable environment, providing opportunities for social interaction and communication, fostering independence and self-advocacy skills, and celebrating the strengths and accomplishments of individuals with Autism. It is also important for families and caregivers to take care of their own well-being and seek support when needed.

The impact of family and caregiver involvement on the success of individuals with Autism cannot be overstated. When families and caregivers are actively involved in promoting inclusion, individuals with Autism have a greater chance of reaching their full potential and leading fulfilling lives.

Advocating for Inclusion: Community Support and Resources

Community support is essential for promoting inclusion for individuals with Autism. It is important for communities to be inclusive, accepting, and supportive of individuals with Autism and their families.

Community support can take many forms, including providing accessible community spaces, offering inclusive recreational programs, organizing awareness campaigns and events, promoting employment opportunities for individuals with Autism, and providing resources and services that meet the unique needs of individuals with Autism.

Resources for promoting inclusion in the community include support groups, advocacy organizations, educational materials, training programs, and service providers that specialize in supporting individuals with Autism. It is important for individuals with Autism and their families to connect with these resources to access the support they need.

Strategies for advocating for inclusion in the community include raising awareness about Autism through education campaigns, challenging stereotypes and misconceptions, promoting inclusive policies and practices, and collaborating with community organizations and stakeholders to create inclusive opportunities for individuals with Autism.

Addressing Mental Health Needs: Supporting Individuals with Autism and Co-Occurring Conditions

Individuals with Autism are more likely to experience co-occurring mental health conditions such as anxiety, depression, ADHD, and obsessive-compulsive disorder. It is important to address these mental health needs in order to promote the overall well-being of individuals with Autism.

Strategies for addressing mental health needs in individuals with Autism include providing access to mental health services, offering individual or group therapy, teaching coping skills and stress management techniques, and creating a supportive environment that promotes emotional well-being.

A holistic approach to treatment is important when addressing mental health needs in individuals with Autism. This includes considering the unique strengths and challenges of each individual, involving families and caregivers in the treatment process, and collaborating with professionals from different disciplines to provide comprehensive support.

Building Self-Esteem and Confidence: Empowering Individuals with Autism

Building self-esteem and confidence is crucial for empowering individuals with Autism. When individuals with Autism have a positive self-image and believe in their abilities, they are more likely to take risks, pursue their goals, and reach their full potential.

Strategies for promoting self-esteem and confidence in individuals with Autism include celebrating their strengths and accomplishments, providing opportunities for success, setting realistic goals, fostering independence and self-advocacy skills, and promoting a positive self-image.

It is important to focus on the unique strengths and talents of individuals with Autism and provide them with opportunities to showcase their abilities. By highlighting their strengths, individuals with Autism can develop a sense of pride and confidence in themselves.

The impact of self-esteem and confidence on the success of individuals with Autism cannot be underestimated. When individuals with Autism believe in themselves and their abilities, they are more likely to overcome challenges, pursue their passions, and lead fulfilling lives.

The Power of Inclusion and the Future of Autism Support

Inclusion is essential for individuals with Autism to reach their full potential and lead fulfilling lives. It promotes acceptance, understanding, and equal opportunities for individuals with Autism in all aspects of life.

The future of Autism support lies in continued efforts to promote inclusion in education, employment, and community settings. This includes challenging stereotypes breed misconceptions, providing accommodations and support, promoting social interaction and communication, accommodating sensory sensitivities, involving families and caregivers, advocating for community support and resources, addressing mental health needs, building self-esteem and confidence, and celebrating the strengths and accomplishments of individuals with Autism.

In conclusion, inclusion is not only a moral imperative but also a practical approach that benefits individuals with Autism and society as a whole. By embracing inclusion, we can create a more accepting and inclusive world where individuals with Autism can thrive. It is up to all of us to promote inclusion in our communities, schools, workplaces, and beyond. Together, we can make a difference in the lives of individuals with Autism and create a brighter future for all.

Chapter 16: Don't Miss These Early Signs of Autism in Your Child

Autism Spectrum Disorder (ASD) is a neurodevelopmental disorder that affects individuals' social communication and behavior. It is characterized by a range of symptoms and challenges, which can vary greatly from person to person. ASD is typically diagnosed in early childhood, although some individuals may not receive a diagnosis until later in life.

The prevalence of ASD has been increasing in recent years, with current estimates suggesting that approximately 1 in 54 children in the United States are diagnosed with ASD. This increase may be due to improved awareness and diagnostic criteria, as well as a better understanding of the disorder.

Early detection and intervention are crucial for individuals with ASD. Research has shown that early intervention can lead to improved outcomes in areas such as communication, social skills, and behavior. By identifying and addressing the early signs of ASD, children can receive the support they need to reach their full potential.

What Are the Early Signs of Autism?

Recognizing the early signs of autism is essential for early detection and intervention. While every child with ASD is unique, there are some common signs and symptoms that may indicate the presence of the disorder.

One of the earliest signs of ASD is difficulty with social communication. Children with ASD may have difficulty with nonverbal communication, such as making eye contact or using gestures. They may also have delayed language development or a lack of interest in social interaction. These challenges can make it difficult for children with ASD to form relationships and engage in typical social interactions.

There are also several common misconceptions about ASD that can make it challenging to recognize the early signs. For example, some people believe that individuals with ASD are not capable of forming relationships or experiencing emotions. However, this is not true. While individuals with ASD may have difficulty with social communication, they are still capable of forming meaningful connections with others.

Social Communication Challenges in Early Childhood

One of the hallmark features of ASD is difficulty with social communication. Children with ASD may struggle with nonverbal communication, such as making eye contact, using gestures, or understanding facial expressions. They may also have delayed language development, speaking later than their peers or having difficulty with speech sounds and grammar.

These challenges can make it difficult for children with ASD to engage in social interactions and form relationships. They may have a limited interest in playing with others or may prefer to engage in solitary activities. They may also have difficulty understanding social cues, such as when someone is joking or being sarcastic.

It is important to recognize these early signs of social communication challenges in order to provide appropriate support and intervention. Early intervention can help children with ASD develop their communication skills and improve their ability to interact with others.

Repetitive Behaviors and Restricted Interests

Another common feature of ASD is the presence of repetitive behaviors and restricted interests. Children with ASD may engage in repetitive movements, such as hand-flapping or rocking back and forth. They may also have a strong attachment to certain objects or routines and become upset if these are disrupted.

These repetitive behaviors can impact daily life for individuals with ASD. They may interfere with their ability to engage in typical activities or interact with others. For example, a child who is fixated on a particular toy may have difficulty transitioning to a new activity or sharing with others.

In addition to repetitive behaviors, individuals with ASD often have restricted interests. They may become intensely focused on a particular topic or subject and have extensive knowledge about it. While this intense focus can be a strength, it can also limit their ability to engage in a variety of activities and interests.

Sensory Sensitivities and Overstimulation

Many individuals with ASD also experience sensory sensitivities and can become easily overstimulated by certain sensory inputs. They may be hypersensitive to sounds, touch, smells, or visual stimuli. For example, they may cover their ears or become distressed in noisy environments, or they may be bothered by certain textures or smells.

These sensory sensitivities can impact behavior and make it challenging for individuals with ASD to navigate their environment.

They may become overwhelmed or anxious in situations that others find tolerable. This can lead to avoidance of certain activities or places, as well as difficulty with transitions and changes in routine.

Understanding and addressing these sensory sensitivities is important for individuals with ASD. By creating a sensory-friendly environment and providing appropriate accommodations, individuals with ASD can better manage their sensory sensitivities and reduce overstimulation.

Delayed Speech and Language Development

Delayed speech and language development is another common early sign of ASD. Children with ASD may speak later than their peers or have difficulty with speech sounds and grammar. They may also have a limited vocabulary or struggle to understand and use language in a meaningful way.

Early intervention is crucial for supporting speech and language development in children with ASD. Speech therapy can help children improve their communication skills and learn strategies for expressing themselves effectively. It is important to provide individualized support that takes into account the unique strengths and challenges of each child.

In addition to formal therapy, there are also strategies that parents and caregivers can use to support language development in children with ASD. These include providing visual supports, using simple and concrete language, and creating opportunities for communication throughout the day.

Lack of Eye Contact and Social Interaction

Difficulty with eye contact is another common challenge for individuals with ASD. Children with ASD may avoid making eye contact or may have difficulty sustaining eye contact during conversations. This can make it challenging for them to engage in social interactions and form relationships.

Eye contact is an important social cue that helps us understand others' emotions and intentions. When individuals with ASD struggle with eye contact, they may miss out on important social information and have difficulty understanding others' perspectives.

Promoting eye contact and social interaction is important for individuals with ASD. Strategies such as using visual supports, providing social stories, and practicing social skills can help individuals with ASD improve their ability to engage in social interactions and form meaningful connections with others.

Unusual Responses to Sounds, Touch, or Smells

Individuals with ASD often have unusual responses to sensory stimuli, such as sounds, touch, or smells. They may be hypersensitive to certain sensory inputs and become overwhelmed or distressed by them. For example, they may cover their ears or become upset in noisy environments.

On the other hand, some individuals with ASD may be hyposensitive to sensory stimuli and seek out intense sensory experiences. They may engage in repetitive behaviors such as spinning or jumping in order to stimulate their senses.

These unusual responses to sensory stimuli can impact behavior and make it challenging for individuals with ASD to navigate their environment. It is important to provide appropriate accommodations and support to help individuals with ASD manage their sensory sensitivities and reduce overstimulation.

Difficulty with Transitions and Changes in Routine

Transitions and changes in routine can be particularly challenging for individuals with ASD. They may become upset or anxious when faced with unexpected changes or when transitioning from one activity to another. This can make it difficult for them to navigate daily life and participate in typical activities.

Having a predictable routine is important for individuals with ASD as it provides a sense of structure and predictability. It can help reduce anxiety and make transitions smoother. Providing visual supports, using timers or schedules, and giving advance notice of changes can all help support individuals with ASD during transitions.

Red Flags to Watch Out For in Infants and Toddlers

Recognizing the early signs of ASD in infants and toddlers is crucial for early detection and intervention. While every child develops at their own pace, there are some red flags that may indicate the presence of ASD.

Some early signs of ASD in infants and toddlers include a lack of social smiling, limited eye contact, delayed babbling or pointing, and a lack of interest in social games. These signs may be subtle and can easily be overlooked, but they are important indicators that further evaluation may be needed.

It is important to seek evaluation if you have concerns about your child's development. Early intervention can make a significant difference in the lives of children with ASD, so it is important to act early if you suspect that your child may be at risk.

Early Intervention for Improved Outcomes

Early intervention is crucial for individuals with ASD. Research has shown that early detection and intervention can lead to improved outcomes in areas such as communication, social skills, and behavior. By identifying and addressing the early signs of ASD, children can receive the support they need to reach their full potential.

There are a variety of interventions available for individuals with ASD, including speech therapy, occupational therapy, and behavioral interventions. These interventions are tailored to the unique needs of each individual and can help them develop the skills they need to succeed.

Families seeking support for their child with ASD can access a variety of resources. There are organizations and support groups that provide information, advocacy, and support for individuals with ASD and their families. It is important to reach out for help and connect with others who understand the challenges of living with ASD.

In conclusion, understanding the early signs of ASD is crucial for early detection and intervention. By recognizing these signs and seeking evaluation, children with ASD can receive the support they need to thrive. Early intervention can make a significant difference in the lives of individuals with ASD, improving their communication skills, social interactions, and overall quality of life.

Chapter 17: From Diagnosis to Support: Resources for Families Living with Autism

Autism is a neurodevelopmental disorder that affects individuals in various ways. It is characterized by difficulties in social interaction, communication, and repetitive behaviors. According to the Centers for Disease Control and Prevention (CDC), autism affects approximately 1 in 54 children in the United States. Understanding autism is crucial for families as it can help them navigate the challenges that come with raising a child with autism and provide them with the necessary support and resources.

Understanding Autism: A Guide for Families

Autism is a complex disorder that manifests differently in each individual. It is important for families to have a clear understanding of what autism is and its characteristics. Autism is a spectrum disorder, which means that individuals can have a wide range of abilities and challenges. Some common characteristics of autism include difficulties with social interaction, communication, sensory sensitivities, and repetitive behaviors.

There are many misconceptions about autism that can lead to misunderstandings and stigma. One common misconception is that individuals with autism lack empathy or emotions. However, this is not true. People with autism may have difficulty expressing their emotions or understanding the emotions of others, but they still experience emotions just like anyone else.

Understanding the autism spectrum is also crucial for families. The spectrum encompasses a wide range of abilities and challenges, from individuals who are nonverbal and require significant support to those who are highly intelligent and may excel in certain areas. It is important to recognize that each individual with autism is unique and may require different types of support.

The Diagnostic Process: What to Expect

Recognizing the signs and symptoms of autism is essential for early diagnosis and intervention. Some common signs of autism include delayed speech or language skills, difficulty making eye contact, repetitive behaviors, intense interests in specific topics, and sensory sensitivities. If you suspect that your child may have autism, it is important to consult with a healthcare professional who specializes in developmental disorders.

The diagnostic process for autism typically involves a comprehensive evaluation by a team of professionals, including psychologists, speech therapists, and occupational therapists. The evaluation may include observations of the child's behavior, interviews with parents and caregivers, and standardized assessments. It is important to be prepared for the diagnostic process and to provide as much information as possible about your child's development and behaviors.

Early diagnosis is crucial for accessing early intervention services, which can greatly improve outcomes for children with autism. Research has shown that early intervention can lead to significant improvements in communication skills, social interaction, and adaptive behaviors. It is important to seek a diagnosis as early as possible so that your child can receive the support they need.

Early Intervention: Why it's Important

Early intervention refers to a range of services and therapies that are designed to support the development and learning of young children with autism. These interventions are evidence-based and tailored to meet the specific needs of each child. Early intervention can have a profound impact on a child's development and can help them reach their full potential.

There are various types of early intervention programs available for children with autism. Some common types include applied behavior analysis (ABA), speech therapy, occupational therapy, and social skills training. These programs focus on teaching children new skills, reducing challenging behaviors, and promoting independence.

Accessing early intervention services can sometimes be challenging, but there are resources available to help families navigate the process. In the United States, the Individuals with Disabilities Education Act (IDEA) ensures that children with disabilities, including autism, have access to appropriate educational services. This includes early intervention services for children under the age of three.

Therapy and Treatment Options for Autism

In addition to early intervention programs, there are various therapy and treatment options available for individuals with autism. These therapies are designed to address specific challenges and promote skill development. Some common types of therapy include speech therapy, occupational therapy, physical therapy, and behavioral therapy.

Speech therapy focuses on improving communication skills, including speech and language development. Occupational therapy helps individuals develop skills for daily living, such as self-care and fine motor skills. Physical therapy focuses on improving gross motor skills and coordination. Behavioral therapy, such as applied behavior analysis (ABA), is a widely used approach that focuses on teaching new skills and reducing challenging behaviors.

It is important to choose the right therapy for your child based on their individual needs and strengths. Evidence-based practices for autism, such as ABA, have been shown to be effective in improving outcomes for individuals with autism. It is important to work with professionals who are trained and experienced in providing these therapies.

Navigating the Education System: Advocating for Your Child

Navigating the education system can be challenging for families of children with autism. It is important to understand your child's rights and advocate for their needs. In the United States, children with disabilities, including autism, are entitled to a free and appropriate public education under the IDEA.

Understanding your child's rights under the IDEA is crucial for ensuring that they receive the support they need in school. This includes having an Individualized Education Program (IEP) that outlines their specific goals, accommodations, and services. It is important to actively participate in the IEP process and advocate for your child's needs.

Working collaboratively with teachers and school administrators is also important for ensuring that your child's needs are met. Building a positive relationship with your child's school team can help facilitate effective communication and problem-solving. It is important to communicate openly about your child's strengths, challenges, and goals.

Creating a Support System: Building a Team of Professionals

Creating a support system is crucial for families living with autism. Building a team of professionals who can provide guidance, support, and services is essential. A multidisciplinary team can include professionals such as psychologists, speech therapists, occupational therapists, behavior analysts, and special education teachers.

Each professional on the team plays a unique role in supporting the individual with autism and their family. Psychologists can provide diagnostic evaluations, therapy, and counseling services. Speech therapists can help improve communication skills. Occupational therapists can address sensory sensitivities and develop daily living skills. Behavior analysts can provide behavior management strategies and teach new skills. Special education teachers can provide academic support and accommodations.

Finding and working with professionals can sometimes be challenging, but there are resources available to help. It is important to seek recommendations from trusted sources, such as other parents of children with autism or healthcare professionals. It is also important to interview potential professionals to ensure that they have the necessary qualifications and experience.

Coping Strategies for Families Living with Autism

Living with autism can have a significant impact on families. It is important for parents and siblings to have coping strategies in place to manage the challenges that come with raising a child with autism. Taking care of your own well-being is crucial for being able to support your child effectively.

Some coping strategies for parents include seeking support from other parents of children with autism, practicing self-care activities such as exercise or hobbies, and seeking professional counseling if needed. It is important to recognize your own limits and ask for help when needed.

Siblings of children with autism may also need support and understanding. It is important to provide them with opportunities to express their feelings and concerns, as well as to have their own interests and activities outside of the family. Siblings may benefit from support groups or counseling services specifically designed for siblings of individuals with autism.

Financial Assistance and Resources for Autism

Raising a child with autism can be expensive, but there are financial assistance programs available to help families. In the United States, Medicaid provides health insurance coverage for low-income families, including services related to autism. The Supplemental Security Income (SSI) program provides financial assistance to individuals with disabilities, including children with autism.

There are also nonprofit organizations and foundations that provide financial assistance and resources for families living with autism. These organizations may offer grants, scholarships, or funding for specific services or therapies. It is important to research and reach out to these organizations to explore the options available.

In addition to financial assistance, there are many resources available for families living with autism. These resources can provide information, support, and guidance. Some common resources include autism advocacy organizations, support groups, online forums, and educational materials. It is important to take advantage of these resources to stay informed and connected.

Community Support: Connecting with Other Families

Community support is crucial for families living with autism. Connecting with other families who are going through similar experiences can provide a sense of understanding and belonging. It can also provide opportunities for sharing information, resources, and strategies.

There are various ways to connect with other families in the autism community. Support groups specifically for parents of children with autism can provide a safe space for sharing experiences and seeking advice. Online forums and social media groups can also be a valuable source of support and information.

It is important to reach out and connect with other families who understand the unique challenges of raising a child with autism. Building a network of support can help alleviate feelings of isolation and provide a sense of community.

Technology and Autism: Apps and Tools for Support

Technology has become an increasingly valuable tool for individuals with autism and their families. There are various apps and tools available that can support communication, social skills, behavior management, and daily living skills.

When choosing technology for your child with autism, it is important to consider their individual needs and preferences. Some apps and tools may be more suitable for certain individuals than others. It is also important to consider the evidence base behind the technology and ensure that it aligns with evidence-based practices for autism.

Examples of helpful apps and tools for individuals with autism include communication apps, visual schedules, social skills apps, and behavior tracking apps. These tools can provide support and structure in various areas of daily life.

Looking to the Future: Preparing for Adulthood with Autism

As individuals with autism transition into adulthood, it is important to plan for their future. This includes considering their long-term goals, independence, and support needs. Transition planning should start early and involve collaboration between the individual, their family, and professionals.

Resources for adults with autism include vocational training programs, supported employment services, and independent living programs. It is important to explore these options and find the best fit for the individual's strengths and interests.

Planning for the future can also involve legal considerations, such as guardianship or power of attorney. It is important to consult with an attorney who specializes in disability law to ensure that all necessary legal documents are in place.

Understanding autism is crucial for families as it can provide them with the knowledge and resources they need to support their child effectively. From understanding the characteristics of autism to navigating the education system and accessing financial assistance, there are many aspects to consider when raising a child with autism. However, with the right support and resources, families can help their child reach their full potential and lead a fulfilling life. Additional resources for support include autism advocacy organizations, support groups, online forums, and educational materials.

Chapter 18: Unraveling the Mystery of Autism Symptoms: Understanding the Signs and Behaviors

Autism is a neurodevelopmental disorder that affects individuals in various ways. It is characterized by difficulties in social interaction, communication challenges, and repetitive behaviors. According to the Centers for Disease Control and Prevention (CDC), autism affects approximately 1 in 54 children in the United States. It is important to understand autism and its symptoms in order to provide appropriate support and interventions for individuals with autism.

What is Autism and What are its Symptoms?

Autism, also known as Autism Spectrum Disorder (ASD), is a complex developmental disorder that affects the way a person perceives and interacts with the world around them. It is a spectrum disorder, which means that it affects individuals differently and to varying degrees. Some individuals with autism may have mild symptoms and be able to live independently, while others may have more severe symptoms and require significant support.

Common symptoms of autism include challenges in social communication, repetitive behaviors, and sensory processing issues. Social communication challenges can manifest as difficulty understanding nonverbal cues, such as facial expressions and body language, as well as difficulty initiating and maintaining conversations. Repetitive behaviors can include repetitive movements, such as hand flapping or rocking back and forth, as well as repetitive speech or echolalia.

Early Signs of Autism in Infants and Toddlers

Early detection and intervention are crucial for individuals with autism. Research has shown that early intervention can greatly improve outcomes for individuals with autism by helping them develop important skills and abilities. There are several early signs of autism that parents and caregivers can look out for in infants and toddlers.

One common early sign of autism is a lack of eye contact. Infants typically begin making eye contact with their caregivers within the first few months of life, but infants with autism may avoid eye contact or have difficulty maintaining it. Another early sign is delayed speech development. While every child develops at their own pace, a significant delay in speech development can be a red flag for autism.

Common Behaviors Associated with Autism

There are several common behaviors associated with autism that individuals may exhibit. One of these behaviors is stimming, which refers to repetitive movements or behaviors that individuals with autism engage in to self-soothe or regulate their sensory experiences. Stimming can include actions such as hand flapping, rocking back and forth, or spinning in circles.

Another common behavior associated with autism is echolalia, which is the repetition of words or phrases that the individual has heard. Echolalia can be immediate, where the individual repeats what they have just heard, or delayed, where they repeat words or phrases from previous conversations or experiences. These behaviors occur because individuals with autism may find comfort and predictability in repetitive actions or sounds.

Sensory Processing Issues in Autism

Sensory processing issues are common in individuals with autism. Sensory processing refers to how the brain receives and interprets sensory information from the environment. Individuals with autism may have sensory sensitivities or sensory seeking behaviors.

Hypersensitivity to certain sounds, textures, or smells is a common sensory sensitivity in autism. For example, a loud noise that may not bother most people could be overwhelming for someone with autism. On the other hand, some individuals with autism may seek out certain sensory experiences, such as spinning or jumping, to help regulate their sensory input.

These sensory processing issues can impact daily life for individuals with autism. They may struggle with going to crowded places or wearing certain types of clothing due to sensory sensitivities. Understanding and accommodating these sensory needs can greatly improve the quality of life for individuals with autism.

Social Communication Challenges in Autism

Social communication challenges are a core feature of autism. Individuals with autism may have difficulty understanding and using nonverbal cues, such as facial expressions and body language. They may also struggle with initiating and maintaining conversations, as well as understanding the social rules and expectations of different social situations.

These challenges can impact social interactions for individuals with autism. They may have difficulty making friends or forming meaningful relationships. It is important to provide support and interventions to help individuals with autism develop their social communication skills and navigate social situations.

Repetitive Behaviors and Routines in Autism

Repetitive behaviors and routines are common in individuals with autism. These behaviors can provide comfort and predictability in a world that may feel overwhelming or confusing to them. Repetitive behaviors can include actions such as lining up toys, arranging objects in a specific order, or following strict routines.

It is important to understand that these behaviors serve a purpose for individuals with autism. They can help them feel in control and reduce anxiety. However, it is also important to help individuals with autism develop flexibility and adaptability, as rigid adherence to routines and repetitive behaviors can limit their ability to navigate new or unexpected situations.

Understanding the Connection Between Autism and Anxiety

Anxiety is highly prevalent in individuals with autism. Research has shown that up to 40% of individuals with autism also have an anxiety disorder. There are several reasons why anxiety is common in autism.

One reason is the social communication challenges that individuals with autism face. Difficulty understanding nonverbal cues and navigating social situations can lead to feelings of anxiety and uncertainty. Additionally, sensory sensitivities and sensory overload can also contribute to anxiety in individuals with autism.

Anxiety can greatly impact daily life for individuals with autism. It can make it difficult for them to engage in social activities, attend school or work, or participate in everyday tasks. It is important to provide support and interventions to help individuals with autism manage their anxiety and improve their overall well-being.

The Role of Genetics in Autism

Genetics plays a significant role in the development of autism. Research has shown that there are certain genetic factors that may contribute to the risk of developing autism. However, it is important to note that genetics is not the sole cause of autism, and there are likely other factors at play as well.

Studies have identified several genes that are associated with an increased risk of autism. These genes are involved in brain development and function. However, it is important to remember that not all individuals with these genetic variations will develop autism, and not all individuals with autism will have these genetic variations.

Environmental Factors that May Contribute to Autism

In addition to genetics, there are also environmental factors that may contribute to the development of autism. Prenatal exposure to certain chemicals, such as pesticides or air pollution, has been linked to an increased risk of autism. Maternal health during pregnancy, such as gestational diabetes or obesity, may also play a role.

It is important to note that these environmental factors are just one piece of the puzzle and do not solely cause autism. The interaction between genetics and the environment is complex and not fully understood. More research is needed to better understand the role of environmental factors in autism.

Diagnosing Autism: What to Expect

The diagnostic process for autism involves a comprehensive assessment and evaluation by a team of professionals, such as psychologists, pediatricians, and speech therapists. The process typically involves gathering information about the individual's developmental history, observing their behavior, and conducting standardized assessments.

The assessments used to diagnose autism may include the Autism Diagnostic Observation Schedule (ADOS), which is a structured observation of the individual's social communication and behavior, as well as the Autism Diagnostic Interview-Revised (ADI-R), which is a structured interview with the individual's caregiver about their developmental history.

It is important to remember that a diagnosis of autism is not a label or a limitation. It is a tool that can help individuals and their families access appropriate support and interventions.

Treatment Options for Autism Symptoms

There are several treatment options available for individuals with autism to help manage their symptoms and improve their quality of life. These treatment options can include behavioral therapy, speech therapy, occupational therapy, and medication.

Behavioral therapy, such as Applied Behavior Analysis (ABA), is a commonly used intervention for individuals with autism. It focuses on teaching new skills and behaviors, as well as reducing challenging behaviors. Speech therapy can help individuals with autism improve their communication skills, while occupational therapy can help them develop skills for daily living and sensory regulation.

Medication may also be prescribed to manage specific symptoms or co-occurring conditions, such as anxiety or attention deficit hyperactivity disorder (ADHD). It is important to work closely with healthcare professionals to determine the most appropriate treatment options for each individual.

Understanding autism and its symptoms is crucial for providing appropriate support and interventions for individuals with autism. Autism is a complex neurodevelopmental disorder that affects individuals in various ways. It is characterized by difficulties in social interaction, communication challenges, and repetitive behaviors.

Early detection and intervention are key in improving outcomes for individuals with autism. There are several early signs of autism that parents and caregivers can look out for in infants and toddlers. Common behaviors associated with autism include stimming and echolalia, which serve a purpose for individuals with autism.

Sensory processing issues, social communication challenges, and repetitive behaviors are common in individuals with autism. These challenges can impact daily life and social interactions. Understanding the connection between autism and anxiety is important, as anxiety is highly prevalent in individuals with autism.

Genetics and environmental factors may contribute to the development of autism. The diagnostic process for autism involves a comprehensive assessment and evaluation by a team of professionals. Treatment options for autism symptoms include behavioral therapy, speech therapy, occupational therapy, and medication.

In conclusion, it is important to understand autism and support individuals with autism in their daily lives. By providing appropriate support and interventions, we can help individuals with autism reach their full potential and lead fulfilling lives.

Chapter 19: Unlocking the Mysteries of Neurodevelopmental Disorders: A Comprehensive Guide

Neurodevelopmental disorders are a group of conditions that affect the development of the brain and nervous system. These disorders typically manifest early in childhood and can have a significant impact on an individual's cognitive, social, and emotional functioning. Examples of neurodevelopmental disorders include autism spectrum disorder, attention deficit hyperactivity disorder (ADHD), intellectual disability, specific learning disorder, communication disorders, and motor disorders.

The prevalence of neurodevelopmental disorders is quite high, with estimates suggesting that they affect approximately 10-15% of children worldwide. This means that millions of individuals and their families are impacted by these conditions. It is crucial to understand neurodevelopmental disorders in order to provide appropriate support and interventions for affected individuals.

Understanding the Causes of Neurodevelopmental Disorders

The causes of neurodevelopmental disorders are complex and multifactorial. While there is no single cause that can explain all cases, research suggests that both genetic and environmental factors play a role in their development.

Genetic factors are thought to contribute significantly to the risk of developing neurodevelopmental disorders. Studies have identified specific genetic mutations and variations that are associated with these conditions. For example, certain genes have been linked to an increased risk of autism spectrum disorder or ADHD. However, it is important to note that genetics alone cannot account for all cases, as many individuals with these genetic variations do not develop neurodevelopmental disorders.

Environmental factors also play a role in the development of neurodevelopmental disorders. Prenatal and perinatal factors such as maternal infections, exposure to toxins or chemicals, and nutritional deficiencies have been implicated in increasing the risk of these conditions. Additionally, social and cultural factors can influence a child's development and contribute to the manifestation of neurodevelopmental disorders.

Types of Neurodevelopmental Disorders

There are several different types of neurodevelopmental disorders, each with its own unique set of symptoms and challenges. Some of the most common neurodevelopmental disorders include:

1. Autism Spectrum Disorder (ASD): ASD is a complex disorder characterized by difficulties in social interaction, communication, and repetitive behaviors. It is typically diagnosed in early childhood and can vary widely in severity.

2. Attention Deficit Hyperactivity Disorder (ADHD): ADHD is a neurodevelopmental disorder characterized by persistent patterns of inattention, hyperactivity, and impulsivity. It can significantly impact a person's ability to focus, organize tasks, and regulate their behavior.

3. Intellectual Disability: Intellectual disability is characterized by significant limitations in intellectual functioning and adaptive behavior. It can range from mild to severe and can affect a person's ability to learn, communicate, and perform daily tasks.

4. Specific Learning Disorder: Specific learning disorder refers to difficulties in acquiring and using academic skills, such as reading, writing, or math. These difficulties are not due to intellectual disability or other factors and can significantly impact a person's educational progress.

5. Communication Disorders: Communication disorders include conditions such as speech sound disorder, language disorder, and social communication disorder. These disorders affect a person's ability to understand or use spoken or written language effectively.

6. Motor Disorders: Motor disorders refer to conditions that affect a person's ability to control their movements. Examples include developmental coordination disorder (DCD) and Tourette syndrome.

Symptoms and Diagnosis of Neurodevelopmental Disorders

The symptoms of neurodevelopmental disorders can vary widely depending on the specific condition and the individual. However, there are some common symptoms that may indicate the presence of a neurodevelopmental disorder. These can include delays in reaching developmental milestones, difficulties with social interaction or communication, repetitive behaviors or restricted interests, problems with attention or impulse control, learning difficulties, and motor coordination issues.

Diagnosing neurodevelopmental disorders typically involves a comprehensive evaluation conducted by a team of professionals, including psychologists, psychiatrists, pediatricians, and other specialists. Diagnostic criteria for each disorder are outlined in the Diagnostic and Statistical Manual of Mental Disorders (DSM-5), which provides guidelines for clinicians to make accurate diagnoses.

Early diagnosis and intervention are crucial for individuals with neurodevelopmental disorders. Early identification allows for the implementation of appropriate interventions and support services that can help improve outcomes and quality of life for affected individuals.

The Role of Genetics in Neurodevelopmental Disorders

Genetic factors play a significant role in the development of neurodevelopmental disorders. Research has identified specific genetic mutations and variations that are associated with an increased risk of these conditions. For example, certain genes have been linked to an increased risk of autism spectrum disorder or ADHD.

Inheritance patterns of neurodevelopmental disorders can vary depending on the specific condition and the genes involved. Some disorders have a clear genetic basis and follow a predictable pattern of inheritance, such as autosomal dominant or recessive inheritance. However, many neurodevelopmental disorders have a more complex genetic basis, with multiple genes and environmental factors interacting to increase the risk.

Genetic testing can be helpful in diagnosing neurodevelopmental disorders and identifying specific genetic mutations or variations that may be contributing to an individual's symptoms. Genetic testing can also provide valuable information about the prognosis and potential treatment options for affected individuals.

Environmental Factors and Neurodevelopmental Disorders

In addition to genetic factors, environmental factors also play a role in the development of neurodevelopmental disorders. Prenatal and perinatal factors can have a significant impact on brain development and increase the risk of these conditions.

Prenatal factors such as maternal infections, exposure to toxins or chemicals, and nutritional deficiencies have been implicated in increasing the risk of neurodevelopmental disorders. For example, maternal smoking during pregnancy has been associated with an increased risk of ADHD and other behavioral problems in children.

Exposure to toxins or chemicals in the environment, such as lead or mercury, can also have a detrimental effect on brain development and increase the risk of neurodevelopmental disorders. Additionally, social and cultural factors, such as poverty or exposure to violence, can impact a child's development and contribute to the manifestation of these conditions.

Treatment Options for Neurodevelopmental Disorders

There is no cure for neurodevelopmental disorders, but there are various treatment options available that can help manage symptoms and improve quality of life for affected individuals. Treatment approaches typically involve a combination of medications, behavioral therapies, educational interventions, and alternative therapies.

Medications can be used to manage specific symptoms associated with neurodevelopmental disorders. For example, stimulant medications such as methylphenidate or amphetamines are commonly prescribed to manage the symptoms of ADHD. Antipsychotic medications may be used to manage aggression or irritability in individuals with autism spectrum disorder.

Behavioral therapies, such as applied behavior analysis (ABA), can help individuals with neurodevelopmental disorders learn new skills and improve their behavior. ABA focuses on identifying and modifying behaviors through positive reinforcement and other techniques.

Educational interventions are essential for individuals with neurodevelopmental disorders to help them reach their full potential. Special education services, individualized education plans (IEPs), and accommodations in the classroom can provide the necessary support for academic success.

Alternative therapies such as dietary interventions, sensory integration therapy, or animal-assisted therapy may also be used to complement traditional treatments for neurodevelopmental disorders. However, it is important to note that the effectiveness of these therapies varies, and more research is needed to determine their efficacy.

Therapies for Managing Neurodevelopmental Disorders

In addition to the various treatment options mentioned above, there are specific therapies that are commonly used to manage neurodevelopmental disorders. These therapies focus on addressing specific areas of difficulty and promoting overall development and functioning.

Speech therapy is often recommended for individuals with communication disorders or difficulties. Speech therapists work with individuals to improve their speech and language skills, including articulation, vocabulary, and social communication.

Occupational therapy focuses on improving fine motor skills, sensory processing, and activities of daily living. Occupational therapists work with individuals to develop skills necessary for independent functioning, such as dressing, feeding, and self-care.

Physical therapy can be beneficial for individuals with motor disorders or difficulties. Physical therapists help individuals improve their strength, coordination, and mobility through exercises and therapeutic techniques.

Applied Behavior Analysis (ABA) is a therapy approach that is commonly used for individuals with autism spectrum disorder. ABA focuses on teaching new skills and reducing problem behaviors through positive reinforcement and other behavior modification techniques.

Lifestyle Changes to Manage Neurodevelopmental Disorders

In addition to formal therapies and treatments, there are lifestyle changes that can be beneficial for individuals with neurodevelopmental disorders. These changes can help support overall health and well-being and may have a positive impact on symptoms.

Diet and nutrition play a crucial role in brain development and functioning. A healthy diet that includes a variety of nutrient-rich foods can support optimal brain function. Some individuals may benefit from specific dietary interventions, such as eliminating certain food additives or allergens, although more research is needed to determine the effectiveness of these approaches.

Exercise and physical activity have been shown to have numerous benefits for individuals with neurodevelopmental disorders. Regular physical activity can help improve mood, reduce hyperactivity, and enhance overall well-being. Engaging in activities such as swimming, biking, or team sports can also provide opportunities for social interaction and skill development.

Sleep hygiene is essential for individuals with neurodevelopmental disorders. Establishing a consistent sleep routine and creating a sleep-friendly environment can help promote restful sleep and improve overall functioning during the day.

Stress management techniques can be helpful for individuals with neurodevelopmental disorders who may experience heightened levels of stress or anxiety. Techniques such as deep breathing, mindfulness, or engaging in relaxing activities can help individuals cope with stress and promote emotional well-being.

Coping Strategies for Individuals and Families Affected by Neurodevelopmental Disorders

Living with a neurodevelopmental disorder can present unique challenges for both individuals and their families. It is important to have strategies in place to cope with these challenges and promote overall well-being.

Support groups can be a valuable resource for individuals and families affected by neurodevelopmental disorders. Connecting with others who are going through similar experiences can provide a sense of understanding, validation, and support.

Counseling and therapy can help individuals and families navigate the emotional and psychological challenges associated with neurodevelopmental disorders. Therapists can provide strategies for managing stress, improving communication, and enhancing coping skills.

Self-care strategies are essential for individuals and families affected by neurodevelopmental disorders. Taking time for oneself, engaging in activities that bring joy or relaxation, and prioritizing physical and emotional well-being can help prevent burnout and promote overall resilience.

Advocacy and education are crucial for individuals and families affected by neurodevelopmental disorders. Advocating for appropriate services, accommodations, and support can help ensure that individuals receive the necessary resources to thrive. Educating oneself about the specific disorder and available treatments can also empower individuals and families to make informed decisions.

Future Directions in Neurodevelopmental Disorder Research

Research in the field of neurodevelopmental disorders is ongoing, with a focus on understanding the underlying causes, developing new treatments, and improving early intervention strategies. Some areas of future research include:

Advances in genetics research are providing valuable insights into the genetic basis of neurodevelopmental disorders. Researchers are identifying new genetic mutations and variations that may contribute to these conditions, which may lead to the development of targeted treatments or interventions.

The development of new treatments and therapies is an area of active research. Scientists are exploring novel approaches, such as gene therapy or stem cell therapy, that may hold promise for the treatment of neurodevelopmental disorders. Additionally, researchers are investigating the potential benefits of alternative therapies, such as music therapy or virtual reality therapy.

There is a growing focus on early intervention and prevention in the field of neurodevelopmental disorders. Early identification and intervention can have a significant impact on outcomes for individuals with these conditions. Researchers are working to develop effective screening tools and interventions that can be implemented during the critical early years of development.

Interdisciplinary collaboration is essential for advancing research and treatment options for neurodevelopmental disorders. Researchers from various fields, including genetics, neuroscience, psychology, and education, are coming together to share knowledge and expertise. This interdisciplinary approach is crucial for gaining a comprehensive understanding of these complex conditions and developing effective interventions.

Conclusion:

Neurodevelopmental disorders are a group of conditions that affect the development of the brain and nervous system. They can have a significant impact on an individual's cognitive, social, and emotional functioning. Understanding the causes, symptoms, and treatment options for these disorders is crucial for providing appropriate support and interventions.

Genetic factors and environmental factors both play a role in the development of neurodevelopmental disorders. Genetic mutations and variations have been identified that increase the risk of these conditions. Environmental factors such as prenatal and perinatal factors, exposure to toxins or chemicals, and social and cultural factors can also contribute to the manifestation of neurodevelopmental disorders.

There are various treatment options available for individuals with neurodevelopmental disorders, including medications, behavioral therapies, educational interventions, and alternative therapies. Additionally, specific therapies such as speech therapy, occupational therapy, physical therapy, and applied behavior analysis (ABA) can help manage symptoms and promote overall development.

Lifestyle changes such as maintaining a healthy diet, engaging in regular physical activity, prioritizing sleep hygiene, and practicing stress management techniques can also be beneficial for individuals with neurodevelopmental disorders. Coping strategies such as support groups, counseling and therapy, self-care strategies, and advocacy and education can help individuals and families navigate the challenges associated with these conditions.

Future research in the field of neurodevelopmental disorders is focused on understanding the underlying causes, developing new treatments, improving early intervention strategies, and promoting interdisciplinary collaboration. Continued progress in research and treatment options offers hope for individuals and families affected by neurodevelopmental disorders.

Chapter 20: Living with Pervasive Developmental Disorder: Stories of Triumph and Resilience

Pervasive Developmental Disorder (PDD) is a term used to describe a group of neurodevelopmental disorders that affect an individual's ability to communicate, socialize, and engage in typical behaviors. PDD is characterized by difficulties in social interaction, communication, and repetitive behaviors. It is a lifelong condition that typically manifests in early childhood and affects individuals throughout their lives.

There are several types of PDD, including Autism Spectrum Disorder (ASD), Asperger's Syndrome, and Childhood Disintegrative Disorder. Each type of PDD has its own unique set of symptoms and challenges. Autism Spectrum Disorder is the most common type of PDD and is characterized by difficulties in social interaction, communication, and restricted and repetitive behaviors. Asperger's Syndrome is characterized by difficulties in social interaction and communication, but individuals with this type of PDD often have average or above-average intelligence. Childhood Disintegrative Disorder is a rare type of PDD that involves a significant loss of previously acquired skills, such as language and social abilities.

Understanding the Challenges of Living with PDD

Living with PDD can present a variety of challenges for individuals and their families. Communication difficulties are a common challenge for individuals with PDD. They may have difficulty understanding and using language, making it challenging to express their needs and wants effectively. Sensory issues are also common in individuals with PDD. They may be hypersensitive or hyposensitive to certain sensory stimuli, such as loud noises or certain textures, which can cause discomfort or distress.

Socialization challenges are another significant aspect of living with PDD. Individuals with PDD may struggle to understand social cues and norms, making it difficult for them to form and maintain relationships with others. They may have difficulty understanding nonverbal communication, such as facial expressions and body language, which can lead to misunderstandings and social isolation. Additionally, individuals with PDD often engage in repetitive behaviors, such as hand-flapping or rocking, which can be comforting to them but may be seen as unusual or disruptive by others.

The Importance of Diagnosis and Early Intervention

Early diagnosis and intervention are crucial for individuals with PDD. Recognizing the signs and symptoms of PDD early on can lead to earlier intervention and support, which can significantly improve outcomes for individuals with PDD. Some common signs and symptoms of PDD include delayed or absent speech, lack of eye contact, difficulty with social interactions, repetitive behaviors, and intense interests in specific topics.

The diagnostic process for PDD typically involves a comprehensive evaluation by a team of professionals, including psychologists, speech therapists, and occupational therapists. The evaluation may include observations of the individual's behavior, interviews with parents or caregivers, and standardized assessments. A diagnosis of PDD is typically made based on the presence of specific criteria outlined in the Diagnostic and Statistical Manual of Mental Disorders (DSM-5).

Early intervention services for individuals with PDD can include a range of therapies and supports tailored to the individual's specific needs. These may include speech therapy to improve communication skills, occupational therapy to address sensory issues and develop daily living skills, and behavioral therapy to address challenging behaviors and teach social skills. Early intervention has been shown to have significant benefits for individuals with PDD, including improved communication skills, increased socialization, and better overall functioning.

Coping Strategies for Individuals with PDD

There are several coping strategies that can be helpful for individuals with PDD in managing their challenges and improving their quality of life. Sensory integration therapy is a type of therapy that focuses on helping individuals with sensory issues learn to process and respond to sensory stimuli more effectively. This therapy can help individuals develop strategies for managing sensory overload or sensitivity.

Cognitive-behavioral therapy (CBT) is another effective coping strategy for individuals with PDD. CBT focuses on identifying and changing negative thought patterns and behaviors. It can help individuals with PDD develop more adaptive coping skills and improve their overall well-being.

Social skills training is also essential for individuals with PDD. This type of therapy focuses on teaching individuals the skills they need to navigate social situations successfully. It can include role-playing, modeling, and practicing social interactions in a supportive environment.

Mindfulness practices, such as meditation and deep breathing exercises, can also be beneficial for individuals with PDD. These practices can help individuals manage stress and anxiety and improve their ability to focus and regulate their emotions.

Support Systems for Families of Individuals with PDD

Families of individuals with PDD often face unique challenges and may require additional support. Parent support groups can be a valuable resource for families, providing a safe space to share experiences, ask questions, and receive support from others who are going through similar situations. These groups can also provide valuable information about resources and services available in the community.

Family therapy can also be beneficial for families of individuals with PDD. This type of therapy focuses on improving communication and relationships within the family system. It can help family members better understand and support each other, navigate challenges related to PDD, and develop strategies for managing stress.

Respite care is another important support system for families of individuals with PDD. Respite care provides temporary relief for caregivers by offering short-term care for the individual with PDD. This can give caregivers a much-needed break and time to recharge.

Financial assistance programs may also be available to families of individuals with PDD. These programs can help offset the costs associated with therapies, medications, and other necessary supports.

Navigating the Educational System with PDD

Navigating the educational system can be challenging for individuals with PDD and their families. However, there are several resources and supports available to help ensure that individuals with PDD receive an appropriate education. Special education services are available in most school districts and provide individualized support and accommodations for students with disabilities. These services may include specialized instruction, assistive technology, and modifications to the curriculum.

Individualized Education Plans (IEPs) are an essential tool for individuals with PDD in the educational system. An IEP is a legally binding document that outlines the individual's unique needs and the supports and services they require to succeed in school. It is developed collaboratively by a team of professionals, including parents or caregivers, teachers, and other relevant school staff.

Accommodations and modifications are also crucial for individuals with PDD in the educational setting. Accommodations are changes made to the learning environment or instructional methods to help individuals access the curriculum and demonstrate their knowledge. Modifications involve changes to the curriculum itself to better meet the individual's needs.

Transition planning is another important aspect of navigating the educational system with PDD. Transition planning involves preparing individuals with PDD for life after high school, including post-secondary education, employment, and independent living. This process typically begins when the individual is around 14 years old and involves setting goals, identifying necessary supports, and developing a plan for achieving those goals.

Employment Opportunities for Individuals with PDD

Finding meaningful employment can be a significant challenge for individuals with PDD. However, there are several resources and supports available to help individuals with PDD find and maintain employment. Job coaching and support services can provide individuals with the skills they need to succeed in the workplace. These services may include job training, assistance with resume writing and job applications, and on-the-job support.

Vocational training programs can also be beneficial for individuals with PDD. These programs provide specialized training in specific industries or trades and can help individuals develop the skills they need to secure employment in those fields.

Self-employment options may also be a viable option for individuals with PDD. Starting a small business or pursuing freelance work can provide individuals with more flexibility and control over their work environment and schedule.

Workplace accommodations are essential for individuals with PDD to succeed in the workplace. These accommodations may include modifications to the physical environment, changes to work schedules or tasks, and additional support from supervisors or coworkers.

Relationships and Socialization with PDD

Building and maintaining relationships can be challenging for individuals with PDD, but it is not impossible. With the right support and strategies, individuals with PDD can develop meaningful connections with others. Social skills development is a crucial aspect of building relationships for individuals with PDD. Social skills training can help individuals learn and practice the skills they need to navigate social situations successfully.

Building and maintaining friendships can be particularly challenging for individuals with PDD. However, there are strategies that can help. Finding common interests and engaging in shared activities can be an effective way to connect with others. Joining clubs or organizations related to their interests can provide opportunities to meet like-minded individuals.

Romantic relationships are also possible for individuals with PDD. Open communication, understanding, and patience are key in navigating romantic relationships. It may be helpful for individuals with PDD to seek support from therapists or counselors who specialize in working with individuals on the autism spectrum.

Family relationships can also be challenging for individuals with PDD, but they are essential for overall well-being. Open communication, understanding, and empathy are crucial in maintaining healthy family relationships. Family therapy can be a valuable resource for families looking to improve their relationships and better understand each other's needs.

Overcoming Stigma and Discrimination

Individuals with PDD often face stigma and discrimination due to misconceptions about their condition. It is important to challenge these misconceptions and advocate for the rights and inclusion of individuals with PDD. Advocacy can take many forms, from educating others about PDD to actively working to change policies and practices that discriminate against individuals with disabilities.

Self-advocacy is also crucial for individuals with PDD. Learning to advocate for their own needs and rights can empower individuals with PDD and help them navigate the challenges they may face in various settings.

Addressing discrimination in the workplace and community is essential for creating a more inclusive society. This can involve educating employers and coworkers about PDD, advocating for reasonable accommodations, and challenging discriminatory practices or policies.

Success Stories of Individuals with PDD

There are many examples of individuals with PDD who have achieved success in various areas of life. These success stories serve as inspiration and hope for individuals with PDD and their families. Some individuals with PDD have excelled in academics, pursuing higher education and careers in fields such as science, technology, engineering, and mathematics (STEM). Others have found success in the arts, sports, or entrepreneurship.

These success stories highlight the unique strengths and abilities of individuals with PDD. Many individuals with PDD possess exceptional attention to detail, strong problem-solving skills, and a unique perspective on the world. By embracing their strengths and finding their passion, individuals with PDD can achieve great things.

Embracing Neurodiversity and Celebrating Differences

In conclusion, Pervasive Developmental Disorder (PDD) is a group of neurodevelopmental disorders that affect an individual's ability to communicate, socialize, and engage in typical behaviors. Living with PDD presents various challenges, including communication difficulties, sensory issues, socialization challenges, and repetitive behaviors.

Diagnosis and early intervention are crucial for individuals with PDD. Coping strategies such as sensory integration therapy, cognitive-behavioral therapy, social skills training, and mindfulness practices can help individuals manage their challenges effectively. Support systems for families of individuals with PDD include parent support groups, family therapy, respite care, and financial assistance.

Navigating the educational system with PDD involves accessing special education services, developing Individualized Education Plans (IEPs), and implementing accommodations and modifications. Employment opportunities for individuals with PDD can be found through job coaching and support, vocational training programs, self-employment options, and workplace accommodations.

Building and maintaining relationships can be challenging for individuals with PDD, but with the right support and strategies, it is possible. Overcoming stigma and discrimination requires advocacy and self-advocacy, as well as addressing discriminatory practices in the workplace and community.

Success stories of individuals with PDD serve as inspiration and hope for those living with PDD. By embracing neurodiversity and celebrating differences, individuals with PDD and their families can find acceptance, support, and opportunities to thrive.

Chapter 21: Breaking Down the Myths: Understanding Autism Spectrum Disorder

Autism Spectrum Disorder (ASD) is a complex neurodevelopmental disorder that affects individuals in various ways. It is characterized by difficulties in social interaction, communication, and repetitive behaviors. Understanding ASD is crucial for promoting inclusivity and providing appropriate support for individuals with ASD and their families. This article aims to provide a comprehensive overview of ASD, debunk common myths, explore the role of genetics, discuss common symptoms and behaviors, highlight the importance of early intervention and therapy, address challenges in social communication, examine the link between ASD and anxiety, challenge misconceptions about empathy, emphasize the importance of embracing neurodiversity and inclusion, and provide resources and support for individuals and families affected by ASD.

What is Autism Spectrum Disorder (ASD)?

ASD is a neurodevelopmental disorder that affects how individuals perceive and interact with the world around them. It is characterized by difficulties in social communication and interaction, as well as restricted and repetitive patterns of behavior, interests, or activities. The severity of symptoms can vary widely among individuals with ASD, which is why it is referred to as a spectrum disorder.

There are different types of ASD, including autistic disorder (classic autism), Asperger syndrome, and pervasive developmental disorder-not otherwise specified (PDD-NOS). Autistic disorder is characterized by significant social, communication, and behavioral challenges. Asperger syndrome is characterized by difficulties in social interaction and nonverbal communication but without significant delays in language or cognitive development. PDD-NOS is diagnosed when an individual does not meet the criteria for autistic disorder or Asperger syndrome but still exhibits some symptoms of ASD.

The prevalence of ASD has been increasing over the years. According to the Centers for Disease Control and Prevention (CDC), approximately 1 in 54 children in the United States has been diagnosed with ASD. This increase may be due to improved awareness and diagnostic criteria, as well as other factors that are still being studied.

Debunking the myth of ASD being caused by bad parenting

Historically, there have been misconceptions and blame placed on parents for causing their child's ASD. This belief stemmed from the idea that cold and unloving parenting styles could lead to the development of ASD. However, scientific evidence has consistently disproven this myth.

Numerous studies have shown that ASD is a complex disorder with a strong genetic component. Research has identified specific genes and genetic variations associated with an increased risk of developing ASD. Additionally, environmental factors, such as prenatal exposure to certain substances or complications during pregnancy or birth, may also play a role in the development of ASD.

The impact of the myth of bad parenting on individuals with ASD and their families cannot be underestimated. It has led to feelings of guilt, shame, and isolation for parents who were wrongly blamed for their child's condition. It is essential to dispel this myth and promote understanding and support for individuals with ASD and their families.

The role of genetics in ASD

Genetic factors play a significant role in the development of ASD. Studies have shown that there are specific genes and genetic variations associated with an increased risk of developing ASD. However, it is important to note that not all individuals with these genetic variations will develop ASD, and not all individuals with ASD have these specific genetic variations.

Genetic testing can be beneficial for families affected by ASD. It can help identify specific genetic variations that may be associated with ASD and provide valuable information for families regarding recurrence risks and potential treatment options. Genetic testing can also aid in early diagnosis and intervention, which is crucial for improving outcomes for individuals with ASD.

The implications of genetic research in ASD are vast. By identifying specific genes and genetic variations associated with ASD, researchers can gain a better understanding of the underlying biological mechanisms involved in the disorder. This knowledge can potentially lead to the development of targeted treatments and interventions tailored to individuals with ASD based on their genetic profile.

Common symptoms and behaviors associated with ASD

Individuals with ASD may exhibit a wide range of symptoms and behaviors. Some common characteristics include difficulties in social communication, repetitive behaviors and routines, sensory processing differences, and other associated symptoms.

Social communication difficulties are a hallmark feature of ASD. Individuals may have difficulty understanding and using nonverbal cues, such as facial expressions and body language. They may also struggle with initiating and maintaining conversations, understanding sarcasm or humor, and interpreting social norms.

Repetitive behaviors and routines are another common feature of ASD. These behaviors can include repetitive movements, such as hand flapping or rocking, as well as rigid adherence to specific routines or rituals. Individuals with ASD may also have intense interests in specific topics or objects.

Sensory processing differences are often observed in individuals with ASD. They may be hypersensitive or hyposensitive to certain sensory stimuli, such as sounds, lights, textures, or smells. These differences can lead to sensory overload or sensory-seeking behaviors.

Other symptoms and behaviors associated with ASD can include difficulties with executive functioning (such as organization and planning), sleep disturbances, gastrointestinal issues, and motor coordination challenges.

Understanding sensory processing differences in individuals with ASD

Sensory processing refers to how the brain receives and interprets sensory information from the environment. Individuals with ASD often have differences in sensory processing, which can impact their daily functioning and overall well-being.

Common sensory processing differences in individuals with ASD include hypersensitivity (over-responsiveness) or hyposensitivity (under-responsiveness) to sensory stimuli. For example, some individuals may be extremely sensitive to certain sounds or textures, while others may seek out intense sensory experiences.

These sensory processing differences can lead to challenges in various environments. For example, a child with ASD who is hypersensitive to loud noises may become overwhelmed in a crowded classroom or a noisy shopping mall. On the other hand, a child who is hyposensitive to touch may seek out intense physical sensations, such as crashing into objects or seeking deep pressure.

Strategies for supporting individuals with sensory processing differences include creating a sensory-friendly environment, providing sensory breaks, and using sensory tools and techniques. Occupational therapy can also be beneficial in helping individuals develop strategies to regulate their sensory experiences.

The importance of early intervention and therapy for children with ASD

Early intervention is crucial for children with ASD. Research has shown that early diagnosis and intervention can lead to improved outcomes in areas such as communication, social skills, and adaptive behavior.

Early intervention can involve a range of therapies and interventions tailored to the individual needs of the child. Some common types of therapy for children with ASD include applied behavior analysis (ABA), speech therapy, occupational therapy, and social skills training.

ABA is a widely used and evidence-based approach that focuses on teaching new skills and reducing challenging behaviors through positive reinforcement and systematic teaching methods. Speech therapy can help improve communication skills, while occupational therapy can address sensory processing differences and help develop daily living skills. Social skills training focuses on teaching appropriate social behaviors and interactions.

Despite the benefits of early intervention, there are challenges and barriers to accessing these services. These challenges can include long waitlists, limited availability of services in certain areas, financial constraints, and lack of awareness or understanding about the importance of early intervention. It is crucial to advocate for increased access to early intervention services for all children with ASD.

The challenges of social communication for individuals with ASD

Social communication refers to the ability to understand and use verbal and nonverbal cues in social interactions. Individuals with ASD often face significant challenges in this area.

Common challenges for individuals with ASD include difficulties understanding nonverbal cues, such as facial expressions, body language, and tone of voice. They may also struggle with initiating and maintaining conversations, understanding sarcasm or humor, and interpreting social norms.

These challenges can lead to social isolation, misunderstandings, and difficulties forming and maintaining relationships. However, with appropriate support and intervention, individuals with ASD can develop social communication skills and improve their overall quality of life.

Strategies for supporting social communication development include using visual supports, such as social stories or visual schedules, providing explicit instruction and feedback, and creating structured opportunities for social interaction. Social skills training programs can also be beneficial in teaching individuals with ASD specific social skills and strategies.

The link between ASD and anxiety

Anxiety is highly prevalent in individuals with ASD. Research has shown that up to 40% of individuals with ASD also meet the criteria for an anxiety disorder. The reasons for this high comorbidity are complex and multifaceted.

Several factors contribute to anxiety in individuals with ASD. The challenges associated with social communication and interaction can lead to feelings of uncertainty and anxiety in social situations. Sensory processing differences can also contribute to anxiety, as individuals may become overwhelmed by certain sensory stimuli. Additionally, the rigid adherence to routines and difficulty with change can lead to anxiety when faced with unexpected or unfamiliar situations.

Managing anxiety in individuals with ASD requires a comprehensive approach. Strategies may include providing a predictable and structured environment, teaching relaxation techniques, using visual supports to reduce uncertainty, and addressing specific fears or phobias through gradual exposure therapy. It is important to work closely with professionals who have experience in both ASD and anxiety to develop an individualized treatment plan.

The misconception of individuals with ASD lacking empathy

There is a common misconception that individuals with ASD lack empathy. However, this belief is not supported by scientific evidence.

Empathy refers to the ability to understand and share the feelings of others. While individuals with ASD may have challenges in expressing empathy in conventional ways, research has shown that they are capable of experiencing empathy.

Studies have found that individuals with ASD may have a different way of processing and expressing empathy. They may have difficulty recognizing and interpreting nonverbal cues associated with emotions, such as facial expressions or body language. However, when provided with explicit instruction and support, individuals with ASD can develop empathy skills and demonstrate care and concern for others.

Understanding and supporting empathy in individuals with ASD is crucial for promoting inclusivity and fostering positive relationships. It is important to provide opportunities for individuals with ASD to learn and practice empathy skills, as well as educate others about the unique ways in which individuals with ASD may express empathy.

The importance of embracing neurodiversity and inclusion

Neurodiversity refers to the idea that neurological differences, such as those associated with ASD, are natural variations of the human brain rather than deficits or disorders. Embracing neurodiversity means recognizing and valuing the unique strengths and perspectives of individuals with ASD.

Embracing neurodiversity and promoting inclusion has numerous benefits. It fosters a more inclusive society where individuals with ASD can participate fully and contribute their unique talents and abilities. It also challenges societal norms and stereotypes about what is considered "normal" or "typical" behavior.

Strategies for promoting neurodiversity and inclusion in society include creating inclusive educational environments, providing reasonable accommodations in the workplace, promoting acceptance and understanding through education and awareness campaigns, and advocating for policies that support the rights and inclusion of individuals with ASD.

Resources and support for individuals and families affected by ASD

There are numerous national and local organizations that provide resources and support for individuals and families affected by ASD. These organizations offer information, advocacy, support groups, educational materials, and other services.

Some national organizations include Autism Speaks, Autism Society of America, Autism Science Foundation, and National Autism Association. These organizations provide a wealth of information on various topics related to ASD, including research updates, treatment options, and support services.

Support groups and online communities can also be valuable resources for individuals and families affected by ASD. These groups provide a safe space for individuals to connect, share experiences, and seek support from others who understand their unique challenges.

Financial and legal resources are also available for individuals and families affected by ASD. These resources can help navigate the complex healthcare and educational systems, access funding for therapies and interventions, and advocate for the rights of individuals with ASD.

Understanding Autism Spectrum Disorder (ASD) is crucial for promoting inclusivity and providing appropriate support for individuals with ASD and their families. ASD is a complex neurodevelopmental disorder characterized by difficulties in social communication, repetitive behaviors, and sensory processing differences. It is important to debunk myths about ASD being caused by bad parenting and recognize the role of genetics in the development of ASD.

Common symptoms and behaviors associated with ASD include social communication difficulties, repetitive behaviors and routines, sensory processing differences, and other associated symptoms. Early intervention and therapy are crucial for improving outcomes for children with ASD, but there are challenges and barriers to accessing these services. Individuals with ASD may also face challenges in social communication, experience anxiety, and be misunderstood in terms of empathy.

Embracing neurodiversity and inclusion is essential for creating a more inclusive society that values the unique strengths and perspectives of individuals with ASD. There are numerous resources and support available for individuals and families affected by ASD, including national organizations, support groups, and financial and legal resources.

In conclusion, it is important to promote understanding and support for individuals with ASD and their families. By challenging misconceptions, providing appropriate interventions, embracing neurodiversity, and accessing available resources, we can create a more inclusive society where individuals with ASD can thrive.

Chapter 22: Breaking the Stigma: Understanding Asperger's Syndrome

Asperger's Syndrome is a neurodevelopmental disorder that affects how individuals perceive and interact with the world around them. It is characterized by difficulties in social interaction, communication, and repetitive patterns of behavior. While it is considered to be on the milder end of the autism spectrum, it can still have a significant impact on the lives of those who have it. Understanding and raising awareness about Asperger's Syndrome is crucial in order to provide support and create an inclusive society for individuals with this condition.

What is Asperger's Syndrome?

Asperger's Syndrome is a developmental disorder that was first identified by Austrian pediatrician Hans Asperger in the 1940s. It is characterized by difficulties in social interaction, restricted and repetitive patterns of behavior, and intense interests in specific subjects. Individuals with Asperger's Syndrome often have difficulty understanding social cues, making eye contact, and engaging in reciprocal conversations. They may also have a strong need for routine and may become upset by changes in their environment.

One key difference between Asperger's Syndrome and other autism spectrum disorders is that individuals with Asperger's Syndrome typically have average or above-average intelligence. They may excel in certain areas, such as math or science, but struggle with social skills and understanding nonverbal communication. This can make it challenging for them to navigate social situations and form meaningful relationships.

The History of Asperger's Syndrome: From Diagnosis to Understanding

Asperger's Syndrome was first described by Hans Asperger in 1944, but it wasn't until the 1980s that it gained recognition as a distinct condition. Prior to this, individuals with Asperger's Syndrome were often misdiagnosed or labeled as having other conditions such as schizophrenia or attention deficit hyperactivity disorder (ADHD).

Over time, researchers and clinicians began to recognize the unique characteristics of Asperger's Syndrome and the need for a separate diagnosis. In 1994, it was included in the fourth edition of the Diagnostic and Statistical Manual of Mental Disorders (DSM-IV) as a separate diagnosis within the autism spectrum. However, in 2013, the DSM-5 merged Asperger's Syndrome with other autism spectrum disorders under the umbrella term "autism spectrum disorder."

The Symptoms of Asperger's Syndrome: What to Look For

The symptoms of Asperger's Syndrome can vary from person to person, but there are some common characteristics that are often present. Individuals with Asperger's Syndrome may have difficulty with social interactions and may struggle to understand social cues and nonverbal communication. They may have a limited range of interests and engage in repetitive behaviors or routines. They may also have difficulty with transitions and changes in their environment.

In addition to these core symptoms, individuals with Asperger's Syndrome may also experience sensory sensitivities, such as being sensitive to loud noises or certain textures. They may also have difficulty with executive functioning skills, such as planning and organizing tasks. These symptoms can impact daily life and relationships, making it challenging for individuals with Asperger's Syndrome to navigate social situations and meet the expectations of others.

Asperger's Syndrome vs. Autism: Understanding the Differences

While Asperger's Syndrome is considered to be on the autism spectrum, there are some key differences between Asperger's Syndrome and other autism spectrum disorders. One of the main differences is that individuals with Asperger's Syndrome typically have average or above-average intelligence, whereas individuals with other autism spectrum disorders may have intellectual disabilities.

Another difference is that individuals with Asperger's Syndrome often have better language skills than those with other autism spectrum disorders. They may have a large vocabulary and speak in a formal or pedantic manner. However, they may struggle with understanding and using nonverbal communication, such as body language and facial expressions.

These differences in intelligence and language skills can impact the diagnosis and treatment of Asperger's Syndrome. It is important for clinicians to consider these factors when assessing individuals for the condition and developing appropriate interventions.

Living with Asperger's Syndrome: Challenges and Coping Mechanisms

Living with Asperger's Syndrome can present a number of challenges in various aspects of life. Socially, individuals with Asperger's Syndrome may struggle to form and maintain relationships. They may have difficulty understanding social cues and may come across as aloof or uninterested in others. This can lead to feelings of isolation and loneliness.

Academically, individuals with Asperger's Syndrome may face challenges in the classroom. They may have difficulty with executive functioning skills, such as organizing their work or managing their time. They may also struggle with sensory sensitivities, which can make it difficult for them to concentrate in a noisy or busy environment.

Professionally, individuals with Asperger's Syndrome may face challenges in the workplace. They may have difficulty with social interactions and understanding workplace dynamics. They may also struggle with changes in routine or unexpected tasks.

Despite these challenges, individuals with Asperger's Syndrome often develop coping mechanisms and strategies to manage their symptoms and improve their quality of life. These may include creating routines and schedules, seeking support from therapists or support groups, and finding outlets for their intense interests.

The Role of Genetics in Asperger's Syndrome

Genetics is believed to play a role in the development of Asperger's Syndrome. Research has shown that there is a genetic component to the condition, as it tends to run in families. However, the exact genes involved are still being studied.

It is believed that multiple genes are involved in the development of Asperger's Syndrome, as well as environmental factors. Researchers are working to identify specific genes that may be associated with the condition in order to better understand its causes and develop targeted treatments.

Understanding the genetic factors that contribute to Asperger's Syndrome is important for diagnosis and treatment. It can help clinicians identify individuals who may be at risk for the condition and provide appropriate interventions and support.

Common Misconceptions about Asperger's Syndrome

There are many misconceptions and myths surrounding Asperger's Syndrome. One common misconception is that individuals with Asperger's Syndrome lack empathy. While it is true that they may struggle with understanding and expressing emotions, this does not mean that they are incapable of empathy. In fact, many individuals with Asperger's Syndrome have a strong sense of justice and fairness and may be deeply empathetic towards others.

Another misconception is that individuals with Asperger's Syndrome are intellectually disabled. As mentioned earlier, individuals with Asperger's Syndrome typically have average or above-average intelligence. They may excel in certain areas, such as math or science, but struggle with social skills and understanding nonverbal communication.

These misconceptions can lead to stigma and discrimination against individuals with Asperger's Syndrome. It is important to challenge these misconceptions and promote understanding and acceptance of the condition.

The Importance of Early Intervention for Asperger's Syndrome

Early intervention is crucial for individuals with Asperger's Syndrome in order to provide them with the support they need to thrive. Early diagnosis allows for early intervention, which can help individuals develop social skills, improve communication, and manage their symptoms.

Early intervention strategies may include social skills training, speech therapy, occupational therapy, and behavior therapy. These interventions can help individuals with Asperger's Syndrome learn how to navigate social situations, communicate effectively, and manage their emotions.

Early intervention also provides support for parents and caregivers, who may need guidance on how to best support their child with Asperger's Syndrome. It can help them understand their child's needs and provide them with the tools and resources they need to support their child's development.

Asperger's Syndrome and Education: Strategies for Success

Education plays a crucial role in the lives of individuals with Asperger's Syndrome. It is important for educators to understand the unique needs of these students and provide appropriate accommodations and support.

In the classroom, individuals with Asperger's Syndrome may benefit from visual supports, such as visual schedules or social stories, to help them understand expectations and routines. They may also benefit from having a quiet space where they can go to when they need a break from sensory stimuli.

Teachers can also help promote social inclusion by fostering a supportive and accepting classroom environment. This can be done by educating classmates about Asperger's Syndrome and encouraging empathy and understanding.

The Future of Asperger's Syndrome Research and Treatment

Research into Asperger's Syndrome is ongoing, with scientists working to better understand the causes of the condition and develop more effective treatments. Advances in genetics research have already provided valuable insights into the genetic factors that contribute to Asperger's Syndrome.

In terms of treatment, there is a growing focus on individualized interventions that take into account the unique strengths and challenges of each individual with Asperger's Syndrome. This personalized approach can help individuals develop the skills they need to succeed in various aspects of life.

There is also a growing recognition of the importance of supporting individuals with Asperger's Syndrome throughout their lifespan. This includes providing support in educational settings, as well as in the workplace and community.

Breaking the Stigma: How to Support Those with Asperger's Syndrome

Breaking down stigmas and stereotypes surrounding Asperger's Syndrome is crucial in order to create an inclusive society for individuals with this condition. This can be done through education and raising awareness about the condition.

It is important to challenge misconceptions and promote understanding and acceptance of individuals with Asperger's Syndrome. This can be done by sharing personal stories and experiences, as well as providing accurate information about the condition.

Supporting individuals with Asperger's Syndrome also involves creating inclusive environments that accommodate their unique needs. This can include providing sensory-friendly spaces, promoting social inclusion, and offering support and resources for individuals and their families.

Asperger's Syndrome is a neurodevelopmental disorder that affects how individuals perceive and interact with the world around them. It is important to understand and raise awareness about this condition in order to provide support and create an inclusive society for individuals with Asperger's Syndrome.

By understanding the symptoms, challenges, and unique strengths of individuals with Asperger's Syndrome, we can better support them in various aspects of life, including education, employment, and social relationships. Early intervention is crucial in order to provide individuals with the support they need to thrive.

Breaking down stigmas and promoting understanding and acceptance of Asperger's Syndrome is essential in order to create a more inclusive society for all. By challenging misconceptions and providing accurate information about the condition, we can help create a world where individuals with Asperger's Syndrome are valued and supported.

Chapter 23: Living with Autism: A Personal Journey of Triumph and Challenges

Autism Spectrum Disorder (ASD) is a neurodevelopmental disorder that affects individuals in various ways. It is characterized by difficulties in social interaction, communication, and repetitive behaviors. ASD is a spectrum disorder, meaning that it affects individuals differently and to varying degrees. Some individuals with ASD may have mild symptoms and be able to live independently, while others may require significant support throughout their lives.

According to the Centers for Disease Control and Prevention (CDC), the prevalence of ASD has been steadily increasing over the years. In 2020, it was estimated that approximately 1 in 54 children in the United States has been diagnosed with ASD. This increase in prevalence has led to a greater understanding of the challenges faced by individuals with ASD and the need for support and resources.

Living with ASD can present a range of challenges for individuals and their families. Some common challenges include difficulties with social interactions, sensory sensitivities, communication barriers, and managing daily routines. These challenges can impact various aspects of daily life, including education, employment, relationships, and overall well-being.

Early Signs and Diagnosis: Navigating the Complexities of Autism Spectrum Disorder

Recognizing the early signs and symptoms of ASD is crucial for early intervention and support. While every individual with ASD is unique, there are some common signs that may indicate the presence of the disorder. These signs can manifest as early as infancy or become more apparent during early childhood.

Some early signs of ASD include delayed or limited speech development, lack of eye contact or social engagement, repetitive behaviors or movements, sensitivity to sensory stimuli, and difficulty with transitions or changes in routine. It is important to note that these signs alone do not necessarily indicate a diagnosis of ASD, but they may warrant further evaluation by a healthcare professional.

The diagnostic process for ASD can be complex and challenging. It typically involves a comprehensive assessment by a team of professionals, including psychologists, pediatricians, and speech therapists. The assessment may include observations of the individual's behavior, interviews with parents or caregivers, and standardized tests. However, diagnosing ASD can be difficult due to the wide range of symptoms and the overlap with other developmental disorders.

Early intervention is crucial for individuals with ASD to maximize their potential and improve their quality of life. Research has shown that early intervention can lead to significant improvements in communication skills, social interactions, and overall functioning. Early intervention programs may include speech therapy, occupational therapy, behavioral interventions, and educational support. These interventions are tailored to the individual's specific needs and can help them develop skills and strategies to navigate daily life more effectively.

Coping Strategies: Finding Ways to Manage Sensory Overload and Social Anxiety

Individuals with ASD often experience sensory overload, which occurs when their senses are overwhelmed by stimuli in their environment.

This can lead to feelings of anxiety, discomfort, and even physical pain. Common triggers for sensory overload include loud noises, bright lights, crowded spaces, and certain textures or smells.

Coping strategies for sensory overload can vary depending on the individual's preferences and sensitivities. Some strategies include creating a calm and quiet space where the individual can retreat when feeling overwhelmed, using noise-canceling headphones or earplugs to reduce auditory stimuli, wearing sunglasses or a hat to minimize visual stimuli, and engaging in deep breathing exercises or other relaxation techniques.

Social anxiety is another common challenge faced by individuals with ASD. They may struggle with understanding social cues, initiating or maintaining conversations, and interpreting nonverbal communication. This can make social interactions stressful and overwhelming.

Coping strategies for social anxiety can include practicing social skills through role-playing or social stories, using visual supports such as social scripts or cue cards to guide conversations, joining social skills groups or therapy sessions to learn and practice social skills in a supportive environment, and seeking professional help, such as cognitive-behavioral therapy, to address anxiety and develop coping strategies.

Support Systems: The Importance of Family, Friends, and Professional Help

Having a strong support system is crucial for individuals with ASD to navigate the challenges they face on a daily basis. Family and friends play a vital role in providing emotional support, understanding, and acceptance. They can help create a safe and inclusive environment where the individual feels valued and supported.

Professional help and therapy options are also essential for individuals with ASD. There are various therapies and interventions available that can help individuals develop skills, manage challenges, and improve their overall well-being. Some common therapies include speech therapy, occupational therapy, applied behavior analysis (ABA), and social skills training. These therapies are tailored to the individual's specific needs and can be highly effective in improving communication, social interactions, and daily functioning.

Building a support network is crucial for individuals with ASD and their families. This network can include family members, friends, therapists, teachers, support groups, and advocacy organizations. Having a support network provides individuals with ASD access to resources, information, and opportunities for socialization. It also helps reduce feelings of isolation and provides a sense of belonging.

Education and Employment: Overcoming Challenges and Achieving Success

Education and employment can present unique challenges for individuals with ASD. In educational settings, individuals with ASD may struggle with social interactions, sensory sensitivities, communication barriers, and difficulties with transitions or changes in routine. These challenges can impact their ability to learn, participate in classroom activities, and form relationships with peers.

However, with the right accommodations and support, individuals with ASD can succeed in education. Accommodations may include visual supports such as schedules or visual cues to help with transitions or understanding expectations, preferential seating to minimize distractions or sensory overload, modified assignments or assessments to meet individual needs, and additional support from special education teachers or aides.

In the workplace, individuals with ASD may face challenges related to social interactions, communication, and sensory sensitivities. However, many individuals with ASD have unique strengths and abilities that can be valuable in the workplace, such as attention to detail, strong problem-solving skills, and a strong work ethic.

Employers can provide accommodations and support to help individuals with ASD succeed in the workplace. This may include providing clear instructions and expectations, allowing for flexible work schedules or breaks to manage sensory sensitivities, providing visual supports or written instructions, and fostering a supportive and inclusive work environment.

There are many success stories of individuals with ASD who have overcome challenges and achieved success in education and employment. These success stories highlight the importance of recognizing and valuing the unique strengths and abilities of individuals with ASD. With the right support and accommodations, individuals with ASD can thrive in educational and work settings.

Relationships: Navigating the Complexities of Love and Friendship

Forming and maintaining relationships can be challenging for individuals with ASD due to difficulties with social interactions, communication, and understanding social cues. They may struggle with initiating conversations, interpreting nonverbal communication, understanding social norms, and forming meaningful connections with others.

However, there are strategies that can help individuals with ASD build and maintain relationships. These strategies include learning and practicing social skills through therapy or social skills groups, using visual supports or social scripts to guide conversations, seeking out shared interests or activities to connect with others, and being open and honest about their needs and challenges.

Communication is key in building and maintaining relationships. Individuals with ASD may benefit from using clear and direct language, asking for clarification when needed, and expressing their thoughts and feelings in a way that others can understand. It is also important for friends, family members, and partners to be patient, understanding, and accepting of the individual's unique communication style.

Advocacy and Awareness: Speaking Out and Making a Difference

Advocacy and raising awareness about ASD are crucial for promoting understanding, acceptance, and inclusion. Advocacy efforts can help challenge misconceptions and stereotypes, fight discrimination, and ensure that individuals with ASD have access to the support and resources they need.

There are many ways to get involved in advocacy efforts. This can include participating in awareness campaigns, sharing personal stories and experiences, volunteering for organizations that support individuals with ASD, attending conferences or workshops on autism, and advocating for policy changes that benefit individuals with ASD.

Advocacy has a significant impact on the ASD community. It helps create a more inclusive society where individuals with ASD are valued and accepted for who they are. It also helps ensure that individuals with

ASD have equal opportunities and access to education, employment, healthcare, and other essential services.

Stigma and Misconceptions: Challenging Stereotypes and Fighting Discrimination

There are many misconceptions and stereotypes about ASD that contribute to stigma and discrimination. Some common misconceptions include the belief that individuals with ASD lack empathy or emotions, that they are intellectually disabled, or that they are incapable of leading fulfilling lives.

These misconceptions can have a significant impact on individuals with ASD. They can lead to social isolation, bullying, discrimination in education or employment, and limited access to support and resources. Challenging these stereotypes is crucial for promoting understanding, acceptance, and inclusion.

Strategies for challenging stereotypes and fighting discrimination include educating others about ASD, sharing personal stories and experiences, promoting positive portrayals of individuals with ASD in the media, advocating for inclusive policies and practices in education and employment, and fostering a culture of acceptance and understanding.

Self-Care: Prioritizing Mental Health and Well-Being

Self-care is essential for individuals with ASD to prioritize their mental health and well-being. Living with ASD can be challenging, and it is important for individuals to take care of themselves and engage in activities that promote relaxation, stress reduction, and overall well-being.

Strategies for practicing self-care can vary depending on the individual's preferences and interests. Some common self-care activities include engaging in hobbies or interests, spending time in nature, practicing mindfulness or meditation, engaging in physical exercise, seeking therapy or counseling, and connecting with others who share similar experiences.

Self-care has a significant impact on mental health and well-being. It helps individuals with ASD manage stress, reduce anxiety, improve mood, and maintain a sense of balance and overall well-being. Prioritizing self-care is crucial for individuals with ASD to thrive and lead fulfilling lives.

Celebrating Differences: Embracing Neurodiversity and Promoting Inclusion

The concept of neurodiversity emphasizes the value of diversity in neurological conditions, including ASD. It recognizes that individuals with ASD have unique strengths, abilities, and perspectives that can contribute to society in meaningful ways. Embracing neurodiversity promotes acceptance, understanding, and inclusion for individuals with ASD.

Strategies for promoting inclusion and celebrating differences include educating others about neurodiversity, challenging stereotypes and misconceptions about ASD, creating inclusive environments that value diversity, providing accommodations and support to individuals with ASD, and fostering a culture of acceptance and understanding.

Inclusion has a significant impact on individuals with ASD and society as a whole. It helps create a more diverse and inclusive society where everyone is valued and accepted for who they are. It also promotes innovation, creativity, and collaboration by embracing different perspectives and abilities.

Living with Autism as a Journey of Triumph and Challenges

Living with ASD is a journey that is filled with both triumphs and challenges. Individuals with ASD face unique challenges in various aspects of daily life, including social interactions, sensory sensitivities, communication barriers, education, employment, relationships, and overall well-being.

However, with the right support, resources, and accommodations, individuals with ASD can overcome these challenges and achieve success. Early intervention, a strong support system, coping strategies, advocacy efforts, and self-care are all crucial components of living a fulfilling life with ASD.

It is important for society to understand and support individuals with ASD. By promoting understanding, acceptance, and inclusion, we can create a more inclusive society where individuals with ASD can thrive and reach their full potential. Together, we can celebrate differences, challenge stereotypes, and make a difference in the lives of individuals with ASD.

Chapter 24: Autism is a neurodevelopmental disorder that affects individuals in various ways, impacting their social interactions, communication skills, and behavior. It is estimated that 1 in 54 children are diagnosed with autism spectrum disorder (ASD) in the United States alone. Early intervention plays a crucial role in supporting children with autism and helping them reach their full potential.

Key Takeaways

Early intervention is crucial for children with autism to improve their social, cognitive, and communication skills.

Parents play a vital role in early intervention by recognizing early signs and symptoms of autism and seeking professional help.

Individualized early intervention plans tailored to the child's needs are more effective than a one-size-fits-all approach.

Nonverbal children with autism can benefit from early intervention strategies such as visual aids and assistive technology.

Overcoming barriers to early intervention, such as lack of access to services and stigma, is essential to ensure all children with autism receive the support they need.

Understanding the Importance of Early Intervention for Autism

Early intervention refers to the services and support provided to children with developmental delays or disabilities at an early age. For children with autism, early intervention is particularly important as it can significantly improve their outcomes later in life. Research has shown that starting interventions as early as possible can lead to better long-term results.

Early Signs and Symptoms of Autism in Children

Recognizing the signs and symptoms of autism at an early age is essential for timely diagnosis and intervention. Common signs include delayed speech or language skills, difficulty making eye contact or engaging in social interactions, repetitive behaviors or restricted interests, sensory sensitivities, and difficulties with transitions or changes in routine.

The Benefits of Early Intervention for Children with Autism

Benefits of Early Intervention for Children with Autism

Improved communication skills

Enhanced social interaction

Increased cognitive development

Reduced behavioral problems

Improved academic performance

Increased independence

Improved quality of life for the child and family

Early intervention programs offer numerous benefits for children with autism spectrum disorder (ASD). These programs focus on improving social skills, communication abilities, academic performance, independence, and self-esteem.

Different Types of Early Intervention Programs for Autism

There are several types of early intervention programs available for children with autism:

1) Applied Behavior Analysis (ABA): ABA therapy focuses on teaching new skills while reducing challenging behaviors through positive reinforcement techniques.

2) Speech therapy: This type of therapy helps improve communication skills by targeting speech articulation difficulties or teaching alternative forms of communication such as sign language.

3) Occupational therapy: Occupational therapists work on developing fine motor skills necessary for daily activities like dressing oneself or holding a pencil.

4) Play therapy: Play-based interventions help enhance social interaction skills by encouraging imaginative play and fostering communication.

How Early Intervention Can Improve Social Skills in Children with Autism

Social skills are crucial for children with autism as they often struggle with social interactions. Early intervention programs provide opportunities for children to learn and practice social skills in a structured and supportive environment. Through targeted interventions, such as group activities or role-playing scenarios, children can develop the necessary skills to engage with others effectively.

The Role of Parents in Early Intervention for Autism

Parents play a vital role in their child's early intervention journey. Their involvement is crucial for the success of the program. Parents can support their child by actively participating in therapy sessions, implementing strategies at home, and advocating for their child's needs.

The Importance of Individualized Early Intervention Plans for Children with Autism

Each child with autism is unique, requiring an individualized approach to intervention. Individualized plans take into account the specific strengths, challenges, and goals of each child. These plans are created collaboratively by professionals working closely with parents to ensure that interventions are tailored to meet the specific needs of the child.

Early Intervention Strategies for Nonverbal Children with Autism

For nonverbal children on the autism spectrum who have difficulty expressing themselves verbally, early intervention strategies focus on alternative communication methods such as sign language or augmentative and alternative communication (AAC) devices like picture exchange systems or speech-generating devices.

The Impact of Early Intervention on Cognitive Development in Children with Autism

Early intervention has a positive impact on cognitive development in children with autism spectrum disorder (ASD). By targeting cognitive skills through various interventions like structured learning activities or problem-solving tasks, early intervention helps improve attention span, memory abilities, executive functioning skills, and overall cognitive development.

XI: The Long-Term Effects of Early Intervention for Children With Autism

The long-term effects of early intervention can be profound for children diagnosed with autism spectrum disorder (ASD). Research has shown that children who receive early intervention services have better outcomes in terms of academic achievement, employment opportunities, and independent living skills. Success stories of individuals who received early intervention highlight the importance of these services in shaping their future.

Overcoming Barriers to Early Intervention for Children with Autism

Despite the benefits of early intervention, there are barriers that can hinder access to these services. Common barriers include limited availability or affordability of interventions, lack of awareness or understanding about autism and its early signs, and challenges in navigating the healthcare system. To overcome these barriers, it is essential to raise awareness about autism and advocate for increased accessibility to early intervention programs.

Early intervention is crucial for children with autism spectrum disorder (ASD) as it provides them with the necessary support and tools to thrive. By recognizing the signs and symptoms at an early age, parents can seek timely diagnosis and access appropriate interventions tailored to their child's needs. With the right support from professionals and active involvement from parents, children with autism can reach their full potential and lead fulfilling lives. It is never too early to intervene; every moment counts on this journey towards a brighter future for children with autism.

In conclusion, early intervention is key in helping children with autism spectrum disorder reach their full potential. By being proactive and seeking help as soon as signs are noticed, parents can ensure their child receives the necessary support and interventions to thrive. With the right resources and guidance, children with autism can make significant progress and lead fulfilling lives. It is important for parents to stay informed, involved, and advocate for their child every step of the way. Every moment counts in the journey towards a brighter future for children with autism, and early intervention plays a crucial role in shaping that future.

FAQs

What is early intervention for children with autism?

Early intervention for children with autism refers to the process of identifying and addressing developmental delays and behavioral issues in children with autism as early as possible. It involves a range of therapies and interventions that aim to improve the child's communication, social skills, and behavior.

Why is early intervention important for children with autism?

Early intervention is important for children with autism because it can significantly improve their long-term outcomes. Research has shown that children who receive early intervention have better communication skills, social skills, and cognitive abilities than those who do not. Early intervention can also reduce the severity of symptoms and improve the child's overall quality of life.

What are some examples of early intervention therapies for children with autism?

Some examples of early intervention therapies for children with autism include applied behavior analysis (ABA), speech therapy, occupational therapy, and social skills training. These therapies are designed to address specific areas of development and behavior and are tailored to the individual needs of the child.

How early should intervention begin for children with autism?

Intervention for children with autism should begin as early as possible, ideally before the age of 2. Early identification and intervention can lead to better outcomes for the child and can help to prevent more severe symptoms from developing.

Who provides early intervention services for children with autism?

Early intervention services for children with autism are typically provided by a team of professionals, including speech therapists, occupational therapists, behavior analysts, and special education teachers. These professionals work together to develop a comprehensive treatment plan that addresses the child's individual needs.

Don't miss out!

Visit the website below and you can sign up to receive emails whenever Travis Breeding publishes a new book. There's no charge and no obligation.

https://books2read.com/r/B-A-CBXDB-YGEXC

Connecting independent readers to independent writers.

Did you love *From Misunderstood To Mainstream*? Then you should read *Celebrating Neurodiversity*[1] by Travis Breeding!

[2]

"Celebrating Neurodiversity" is not just a book; it's a manifesto for acceptance, understanding, and inclusivity. Breeding passionately advocates for the celebration of differences, urging readers to embrace the mosaic of neurodiversity that enriches our society. Through empowering stories of resilience, creativity, and innovation, Breeding showcases the immense potential that lies within the neurodivergent community.

From the unique ways in which neurodivergent individuals perceive the world to the invaluable insights they offer, "Celebrating Neurodiversity" is a thought-provoking exploration of what it truly means to be neurodivergent. Breeding's empowering narrative inspires

1. https://books2read.com/u/4DnjxP

2. https://books2read.com/u/4DnjxP

readers to challenge preconceived notions, foster empathy, and champion diversity in all its forms.

Whether you're a neurodivergent individual, a caregiver, or simply curious about the intricacies of the human mind, "Celebrating Neurodiversity" is a must-read that will leave a lasting impact. Join Travis Breeding on a journey of self-discovery, acceptance, and celebration as we embrace the kaleidoscope of neurodiversity and revel in the beauty of our differences.

Read more at breedingautismconsulting.com.

Also by Travis Breeding

Harmony in Flux: Navigating Bi-Polar Brilliance

The Friendship Rainbow

The Great Kindergarten Adventure: A Story about Going to School with Autism

The Magic Forest Adventure

Unlocking Brilliance: Navigating Autism and Applied Behavior Analysis Towards a Radiant Future

Decoding Love: Navigating Dating and Relationships on the Autism Spectrum

Echoes of a Late Diagnosis: Unveiling the Spectrum Within

From Theory to Practice: Implementing Effective Autism Interventions St

The Amazing Adventures of Aiden and His Asperger's Superpowers

The Magical Adventures of Lily and the Enchanted Forest

Unlocking Potential: A Journey Of Discovery Through ABA Therapy

Unlocking Potential: Navigating Employment for Neurodiverse Talent

Unlocking the Spectrum: A Journey through Applied Behavior Analysis from an Autistic Perspective

Unlocking The Spectrum: Navigating The Complexity Of Autism With Advanced Strategies And Insights

Beyond The Spectrum: Insights From Autistic Adults

Beyond The Stereotypes

Breaking Barriers: Navigating Autism With Therapeutic Insight

Celebrating Neurodiversity

Embracing Differences
From Diagnosis To Treatment
From Dreams To Reality: The Young President
Living With Autism: A Journey Of Triumph And Challenges
Neurodiversity Unveiled: Navigating The Spectrum Of Inclusion
Sunshine At Disney World
The Art Of Reinforcement
The Magical School Bus Ride: A Journey Of Understanding
ThroughThe Spectrum Of Love
From Misunderstood To Mainstream

Watch for more at breedingautismconsulting.com.

About the Author

Travis is the author of over 50 books about autism spectrum disorder. He travelst he country sharing the mission of making the world a better place for autistic individuals. In his spare time Travis enjoys writing, walking, and watching sports.

Read more at breedingautismconsulting.com.